PRECIOUS CHILD
COME FOLLOW ME

PRECIOUS CHILD COME FOLLOW ME

Phyllis A. Amelio

iUniverse, Inc.

New York Lincoln Shanghai

PRECIOUS CHILD COME FOLLOW ME

iUniverse books may be ordered through booksellers or by contacting:

iUniverse
2021 Pine Lake Road, Suite 100
Lincoln, NE 68512
www.iuniverse.com
1-800-Authors (1-800-288-4677)

ISBN-13: 978-0-595-42993-6 (pbk)
ISBN-13: 978-0-595-87336-4 (ebk)
ISBN-10: 0-595-42993-9 (pbk)
ISBN-10: 0-595-87336-7 (ebk)

Printed in the United States of America

"Precious Child Come Follow Me", was written to show how powerful prayer is in each ones life. God our father has a master plan for us to follow, and this is what I have been doing all my life. This also was written to share with you what my life was like growing up during a very stressful time of the Second World War.

With God on my side, I survived the years of growing up during the depression era without a mother to be at my side. Born in New England during the 1930's, many challenges were presented, because I did not know my grandparents very well, I wanted to be a good mother and grandmother. Marriage was on my mind during my high school years as the main goal of my life.

Family life was very important to me, seeing mine was empty in my younger years, my journey path took me to many adventures.

My appreciation goes to my dear friend Ruth Porter for her endless patience and assistance in preparing this manuscript. I am thankful to have had my first helping hand from my sister Patty Ann La Rose Burden, also all the prayer support from my spiritual friends all these years to preserve in my writing.

I also want to thank my daughter, Diane who put the finishing touches into this book.

Contents

I AM GOD'S PRECIOUS CHILD

Who I am I? First of all, I am a child of GOD. I am on this earth to do the work that GOD wants me to do. I am glad that the LORD has chosen me to live here for over seventy years, I am somewhat retired from the job world. I do have time to do my favorite things and one is writing this book. One of my rewarding works was teaching children at church with classes on the life of JESUS and learning about our faith. This filled me with joy each week I was there with the first graders who were just starting to get to know how to pray. God has been so good to me in many ways on my path of life. He has given me so many good friends and family. One path that I have followed was to pray with a group of women I met 34 years ago and we meet monthly for prayer and sharing which has kept our friendship growing and close to the LORD. We also have a chain prayer if someone has a need we call each other so we are aware of each other always. We place our troubles in God's hands for he has the Master plan for us all. We are all on a journey which is planned by GOD so this is my story of how important our efforts are with living a good life connected with our heavenly father for he said: Seek first the kingdom of GOD for it is ours for ever and ever. In life we have many paths to follow. With GOD on our side, we can be happy and successful. Only GOD knows the chosen time for us to return to his loving arms.

GOD'S PLAN FOR ME

God's master plans for me was started on OCTOBER 4th 1936, this was the day the LORD chose for me to be born into a time of hardships for many people for this was the depression years in our country. My father was having a rough time providing for our family. My mother was sick a lot. She spent most of my growing years in the hospital; she suffered with epilepsy which is a neurological disorder that causes recurring seizures. No cure or medication was known at this time. I saw her take spells. She only came home on weekends and holiday visits. Even with all of this, she had another child when I was seven. This was my sister Patty. My grandmother came and took over for she knew that my sister Doris who was only 12 could not take care of this new baby. Patty went to live with my grandmother who had two daughters living with her at the time. This lasted for three years and then my grandmother came to live with us. My father was in business for himself. He was a roof and chimney man. This was very hard work but he was good at it. His days were long but he found time to hit the bars on his way home. He would not come home until very late. So we were home alone a lot. My older brothers tried working for my dad but he was hard to get along with. With the drinking problem this did not help matters either. My oldest brother Arthur was the first to leave, for he joined the army when he was seventeen. He made his own life. My other brother Bob left school when he was sixteen to work with my dad but that did not last long either. So he eventually went away also. My sister said he was in and out of trouble most of the time. Dad would not help him. At least my sister was like a mom to me. Our life really changed when my dad purchased a big old house in the middle of the city of WORCESTER, MASS. It had 17 rooms in it but it needed work which my dad could do himself which he did. This is when my grandmother came to live with us and our two aunts too. My grandmother could see that my father needed help so this is how Patty came to live with us now. My grandmother was a very religious woman, so she saw that we went to church on Sundays. My dad did not go then. His mother was there daily and she taught us to pray the Rosary everyday. We could not go out to play until we prayed first. My faith was taking shape by my grandmother's good deeds. When I was seven she was the one who saw that I had a nice first communion dress for the day I first met JESUS in my soul. This stood out in my mind that she wanted the best for me on this special day. God sent her to us so we would have good care. She raised 17 children of her own so she knew what needed to be done with us. I went to a Catholic school which was right down the street called Holy Family. I attended there from third to eighth grade, which I learned a lot about my faith. It was hard for me but I got through it and graduated from there.

Most of the time my Father was so wrapped up in his own life that he did not know what I was doing a lot of things on my own. While my grandmother was living with us a lot of Dad's family were coming and going all the time. Dad would drink heavily after work. He would stay in the bars till late at night. Grandmother did not like this at all. She and Dad had a disagreement so she decided to get an apartment of her own. She wanted to take me and my sister with her, but I wanted to stay with my Dad. Then my sister Doris left to get married. This was very hard on me for it was like my Mother leaving again. I had many lonely days ahead of me. But on Sundays I would go to the movies and lose myself in the stories. This was my life of make believe. My Dad's drinking problem was not easy to deal with. I just hoped he would go to bed and sleep it off.

My Dad had a girlfriend named Emily. I don't know where he met her but he wanted her to move into our house even though my Mother was living at the hospital. Emily wanted to help my Father with his business. She said that it would be easier for her to do that if she stayed at the house. She did have her own room but it still wasn't right. Emily was a hard working woman. She worked all day in the silk mill and then came home and cooked and cleaned for us. She really loved my Dad. He did slow down on his drinking for awhile. He seemed happy with this arrangement. Emily helped me get through my high school years. I knew that my Dad could not get married because my Mom was still around. Emily was good to her when she came home but I'm sure it hurt her knowing that my Father had a girlfriend living there. My Mom was sad when she went back to the hospital after a weekend at home.

My high school days were happy for me because I made some new friends. I was working with small children. I was training as a nursery school aide and helper. When I was at school I forgot what was happening at home. During high school I attended religious instructions on my own for it meant a lot to me to learn more about my faith. During Lent I offered up my fasting so I would make the right decision on what to do with my life after I graduated from high school.

Just before graduation a concert came to Holy Cross College starring Perry Como. All the girls were going. We were very excited that he was coming. The concert was scheduled to take place on the weekend that I was to go to see my Mother at the hospital. So I decided to go to see my Mom the next weekend. I didn't know that my Mom was having any other health problems. We had a wonderful time at the concert. This was the chance of a lifetime. I thought. The next Sunday I got ready to go see my Mom. I was at the bus stop when Emily came to me and told me not to go that my Mom was very sick with an infection. I felt really sad for I realized that I didn't see her last week and now I wasn't going to see her this week either. That night my Mother passed away. This was a good thing for now my Mother was at peace. No more pain and suffering. She had been in the hospital for many years suffering with her illness. Everyone said that it was a blessing. My Father wanted a private funeral because hardly anyone visited her all these years and now they will not just come to see her now. Only family ever came to see her. Because of the cost, she had been in a state hospital. My sister and I went to see her but it was a bad experience for us. We had to go through locked doors just to visit with her. Most everyone there was mentally ill but we wanted to see her; so we went anyway. We were very fearful of those visits. Now she was at peace and we were happy for her. God had called her to her journey's end. I know I carried a heavy heart because I missed that visit with her on the week of the concert.

I did not think I could get happy over graduation because it was so close to my Mother's death but somehow I got through it. I was surprised when my Dad came, for he never went before Emily made him realize that this was the right thing to do. Doris also came for my big night. I was in a white cap and gown. I was all a glow for I had made it! This was a night of long speeches and awards. I was glad to have completed everything that I needed to finish school yet I would be missing all my friends who would be going onto jobs too. I knew I was ready to start my new life, wherever it would be. We had to say goodbye to teachers that we had for four years. Some of my friends even got married. I didn't date much in high school. I went to an all girls' school. The school offered me a job for the summer working with a mentally retarded girl who needed personal attention with her everyday stuff. Her Mother had been very ill so she needed someone to help her. She was better now but she still needed to rest. I said that I would give it a try for the summer. Maryann was fourteen with the mind of a seven year old. This gave me a chance to use my teaching skills. In my heart something was missing for I really wanted to work with little children.

One day I was checking the want ads in the newspaper, an ad caught my eye. A family was looking for a person who had experience working with little children. This was also a live-in job. I talked to the employment agency and they said that I could get an interview with all the experience I had gotten in school. My teachers gave me a good reference. I prayed that this would work out for it was what I wanted to do. I would have to move away from home to take this job. I was happy just being offered a job with rich people. By the weekend, I made the trip to meet with the Gannett family. When I saw how large and how beautiful their home was, I was so excited. Mr. and Mrs. Gannett talked to me for a long time about all the things the school had said about me. They had three little boys and it would be my job to take care of them when Mrs. Gannett went golfing, or whatever, without the children. They showed me where my room and bath would be. We talked about my working hours. I would work six days a week with every other weekend off. This was just fine with me. I was to start at forty dollars a week plus room and board. It was all part of the deal. I said that I had to talk it over with my Dad and I would get back to them. I was so excited! It was just what I was looking for. I would finally be on my own. This was the answer to my prayers. I talked to my Dad and he said that it was alright with him. I would start my new life in the fall. I had to give notice at my other job so that they could get a replacement for me. I just felt that this was the right thing to do. Because I did a good job at school, they had me on a list as being good with children. I finished my work at my first job and then packed my stuff to move to my new home. I would be on my own but yet I would be with a family. My Dad would be with Emily by himself now.

After I left home Dad started drinking again. Emily could not stand it anymore so she got her own place and moved out. I prayed many years for my Dad to stop drinking and to go back to church. This did not happen till many years later. It took 17 years of prayers before my Dad met a woman of great faith and he did come back to the church. He was faithful for many years after marrying this new person in his life.

Emily died of cancer several years later. She had really tried her best with Dad but he was not able to give up drinking. You could not blame her for that. I stayed with the Gannett family for two and a half good years. I was able to buy an old car of my own. This is why when I decided to leave them it was like leaving my own family for this is what they became to me. God was so good to let all those doors open for me. I was nineteen when I started out on my own again. This is in the next chapter of my journey. Praise the LORD.

THE GREAT HUSBAND HUNT WAS ON

My life with the Gannett family had been really good for two and a half years working as a nursemaid to their children, but I did not have much time to be with people my own age. I really had a hard time telling Nancy and Bill that I had to give up my job. They had been very good to me. I loved the children and I knew it would be hard on them also, but I knew that I wanted a husband and children of my own. I knew I was not going to find a husband in the small town of Hopedale, Massachusetts.

After talking to Bill and Nancy, they agreed that it is hard to get a date when you only have one day a week off. I literally had no social life of my own. One thing they asked of me was would I wait until the end of summer to leave. We all were going to the beach house in New Hampshire. It would be hard to replace me on such short notice. It was fine with me as I loved the beach. I had been praying about a decision to move on and find a new job and hopefully a husband.

Little did I know that the Lord had "all the doors open" for me to go to Florida. While working at the beach house, I met up with Dorothy Bailey, an older woman who was working there as the cook. We became good friends. I told her that I always wanted to go to Miami, Florida. She said that she was to St. Petersburg, which is on the Gulf side, but that she would like to go to Miami also. She asked me what kind of work I would be doing. I told her that I like to work with children, putting down new roots.

All summer we planned for our trip. We would share expenses, with me driving my new 1955 Plymouth, which Mr. Gannett helped me purchase from a local dealer. And now I'm leaving them? Up to this point, I had no living expenses other than gas for the car. Did I realize what I was getting into?

Every Sunday I took Dorothy to church in my new car. We had time to share our friendship and our love of the Lord. I feel that the Lord used Dorothy as an instrument to make my big decision to go to Florida. I remember it being a beautiful summer and somehow I think they thought that I would change my mind about going to Florida, as I enjoyed working with their children so much. My life with this family was so good. Mrs. Gannett understood how much I wanted to have a husband and family of my own. She wanted me to be happy.

I was young and filled with such wonderful dreams of Florida and what it would be like living there; no snow, no cold winters, swimming every day at the beach. We came back home to Massachusetts after Labor Day. I was planning on going to Florida within the next two weeks. Dorothy and I had picked our date to go so I had to get everything ready for my big move. It would be sad leaving the Gannett family as we had grown so close. I was going to a place I had never been before. The Gannetts' told me that I would always have a home with them if I wished to return.

I was excited to get started on our trip. At this time a trip from New England to Florida was a good five days drive plus resting along the way. Dorothy was a woman who was very happy and easy to get along with. We joked around a lot too. We also had to travel on Route 1, for this was the interstate at this time, once we got past the Carolinas. Route 1 was along the coast line. We enjoyed the ride. This was a new experience for me, driving this far away from home. When we finally hit Miami we had to look for a hotel to stay in. The streets were lined with palm trees; and coconuts were lying on the ground! It was so different. It was like living in another world. But it was also very hot and the humidity was high. We did find a nice hotel in our price range. It was off season so there was a lot to pick from and it was the right price. In the winter, this place would be triple the cost.

Dorothy was having trouble with the heat for she had high blood pressure and she had to stay out of the sun. After settling in, I began to look for a job. I knew that I would have to work in order to stay here. I just thought that it was great to have the sun, flowers, palm trees, and little showers here and there all the time. Living by the beach was great too. I went swimming every day. We also had a pool indoors. One day I was playing ball with a couple of children who were in the pool with their mother. She took note of how much fun we were having. We started to talk about why I was here and that I was looking for a job with children. She told me that she was looking for someone to watch her children. She said that she would talk to her husband and then get back to me. This sure sounded good to me as I would be living with a family again.

It was a good thing that I found this job, as Dorothy was having trouble with the heat and wanted to go back home. She asked me if I was sure that I wanted to stay there by myself. I told her about the job with this family. I really wanted to make a go of it here. She got her wish to see Miami but she didn't want to risk getting sick. I understood, but I was going to miss her. I was thinking that now I will be on my own. Little did I know that this was not going to last very long.

Everything was 'nice and rosy," so I thought. It only lasted two weeks when her husband's mother died and the family had to leave to go north because of her death. I had to look for a new place to live and a new job.

I was looking in the paper for a job with children. My funds were getting low. I had a car payment plus rent and food. I was really praying up a storm for I didn't know what to do. I did find a hotel that rents rooms by the week. There were a lot of young people my own age staying there. One day I was checking the paper and saw an ad for a job helping in a nursery school, which is what I did in high school. I got an interview right away as I had experience at this. It was very hard for a snow bird to get a job because they think you are going to leave after the season, which a lot of people did. Once I got settled in my room, I went to talk to the director of the nursery school. It was only part-time but I said I would do it. I needed the work. I worked in the mornings and then hit the beach in the afternoon. It gave me a chance to meet new people who were hanging around just like me.

At least half of my prayers were answered. I missed Dorothy. She kept my spirits up. We had a lot of fun together. I didn't want her to get sick from the heat so I understood why she had to go back. The hotel I was in had a room in the basement that had a refrigerator that we could use. There was also a little stove for cooking to help keep expenses down. I did buy the basics, bread, milk, cereal, fruit, eggs, and pancake batter. I thought my food would be safe down there. But there were also real cheap rooms down in the basement. Guess who took these rooms? Young men my age! They were on vacation and had a very low budget. Little did I know that these guys were hungry and would steal my food. They stole my food while I was out working. These were the same guys that sat on the front porch watching the girls go by. God has a sense of humor but he used this plan for me to meet these men. I would start cooking and they would smell it and come down saying "oh that smells so good," hoping to get some. This is how I met Ray and Joe from Pa. I found out that they were the ones taking my food.

Ray was working a job painting houses. One night Ray asked me out on a date. He seemed like a nice guy, so I said yes. His friend Joe was engaged to a girl back home. He called her collect every night. Everyone was counting their pennies. We were all in the same boat, trying to make a go of it down here. I had a car so we used my car to go places. I liked the attention that Ray was giving me. We would meet on the beach after work. We did things that didn't cost much for we didn't have much money. There was a young married couple staying at the hotel who was trying to make a go of it also. It's hard to start here because everyone who has jobs open thinks you are going to go back home. At night we would all sit out and talk on the porch of the hotel. This is how we got to know each other. I still only had a part-time job and knew I couldn't stay there much longer so I started looking for an apartment to rent. I was enjoying my job but it was not enough money to keep going. I was praying what to do next. Even though I was moving to an apartment, Ray wanted to keep seeing me. I said OK.

I fell in love with Ray. He was a quiet person and we liked the same things. We spent a lot of time together when we weren't working. Finally, one night, Ray asked me to marry him. I was very excited. I said "yes." Ray gave me a small ring but I didn't care. I was engaged! Joe had left to go back home but Ray stayed to be with me. We visited the hotel to see the Cohen's, the young couple we met from New York, who were getting homesick also. So far I had been keeping up with my car payments … but it was hard. Ray said he wanted me to meet his family in Pennsylvania. I said that I would like that for I would not get married down here anyway. We would have to work awhile to save some money. Ray agreed that it would be a good idea to head home. We didn't seem to be making any headway here. We decided to take the Cohen's north with us to share expenses. Also, we would be chaperoned for our trip. This was good for me as I was old fashioned about being alone in the car with Ray at this time. So our plans were in motion. We planned to get home in time for Thanksgiving; I would be doing all the driving as it was my car. We had to give notice to our jobs. Getting packed did not take long. The day we left Florida a cold spell had set in. We picked up the Cohen's from the hotel and were on our way. We were all happy to be going home to see our families and friends. We only stopped for breaks as we couldn't afford a hotel as our funds were low. We finally got to New York before lunch time. The Cohen's invited us to stay for lunch with their family. Everyone was glad to see the newlyweds home safe and sound. Ray and I were only three hours from home so we left in hopes of getting to Bethlehem before dark. Ray called his mother to tell her we were on our way. He also told her we were engaged to be married. It was Thanksgiving night so there was plenty of turkey waiting for us to eat. I was very excited to see where Ray lived and to meet his family. Ray's mother welcomed us in. She had not seen Ray for several months and here he was bringing a stranger into her home. It was a lot to take at one time. His mother seemed to take our news quite well. After we got settled in, she showed me to Ray's sister's bedroom to sleep. We would be sharing her room. This was fine with me. I had a roof over my head for I did not have money for a hotel. I was glad to be able to rest after that long trip. I was happy being with Ray too. I was wondering what we would do next regarding our wedding plans. Ray seemed to be happy to be home with his family again. I really felt that I was in love with Ray so I was happy. Did I really know what love was? Time would only tell and so it did. We were home only a short time when things began to change with Ray. Once he got home and saw his buddies, he started going out with them and partying too much. I would not want to marry anyone who was drinking as much as he was, so Ray and I broke up. I moved out of Ray's house within a couple of weeks and moved into a rooming house. I was looking for a job and couldn't afford an apartment. I didn't want to take advantage of Ray's mother.

I met Ray's friend Joe, who was in Florida with us. He was sorry that we broke up so soon. I told him it was for the best and that I was ready to go back home to Massachusetts. He asked me to wait a little while longer. He also wanted me to meet his girlfriend Maryann. She had just lost her roommate and she needed someone to share her apartment. This worked out for me as I was lonely and needed a place to stay. I moved in with Maryann and we hit it off right away. This is how we all got together. Maryann had a good job and she was saving up to marry Joe. They had made wedding plans a year ahead. I had gotten a job in the Candy Factory, which was not easy work, but it was a job. I was up at 5 am to start work at 6 am. I did not like the job I had and I told Joe that I was still thinking of going home. Again he asked me not to go yet. He said he had someone he wanted me to meet. He also said that a job as a waitress had opened up at a restaurant he goes to. He said that they would train me. I had never worked as a waitress before. So I agreed to try. I was happy living with Maryann and Joe kept saying he had this friend of his that he wanted me to meet but for some reason or other we just couldn't get together. So I talked of going home again. Joe begged me to stay and meet his friend. He was going to set something up real soon. Maryann said that she knew him and he was worth waiting for. Finally that night came. He asked his friend to come to his apartment so that we could meet there. He didn't want a blind date. He wanted to meet me first. I agreed with that. I preferred that we double date the first time anyway. I met Bob with Joe and Maryann there to break the ice. We had fun that night and he asked me out on a real date to go to the movies on Saturday night. Yes—this is how it all happened. We began our relationship by being friends.

Sometimes Bob would come for dinner. He found out that I knew how to cook. You know that old saying "you can reach a man through his stomach." We also liked a lot of the same things. After we had a few dates, Maryann asked me how I liked Bob. I told her I liked him alright but that I didn't know if he would be someone I would want to marry. Little did I know that God had other plans. As time passed by we spent more and more time together. I remember the first time I went to meet his family. I was scared; that's for sure. He came from a family of nine. In those days I was quiet and shy. I was invited to Sunday dinner, which was a little over-powering, to meet them all at the same time. All of his family spoke Spanish because his mother could not speak English. But I got through it ok. I thought it was wonderful to have so much family getting together for a meal. They all seemed so loving to each other. I remember going on a double-date with Bob's sister and her fiancée. We were going to this big night club in New Jersey. I wanted to look real nice so I saved money to get a special dress. I had never been to a night club before. We were going in the same car for this place was about 45 minutes away. The big night came and it was really neat. John and Angie loved to dance and were good at it too. We had a good time but it took us a long time to get home as it was foggy. Angie was really worried for she had to be home before midnight or her mother would be really angry. Even though she was out with us she still had to be on time. We just made it! Even being engaged to John didn't make any difference. Rules were rules.

Bob and I dated all winter long, I was getting very attached to him. I missed him when he had to work and couldn't come over. Summertime came and we went on a lot of cook outs with his family. On the Fourth of July they planned on going to their favorite park to celebrate. Bob was to pick me up at 11 am. I was almost ready when Bob came in and told me he wanted to give me something. He made me close my eyes. He put a little box in my hand and asked me to marry him. I said YES. He took the engagement ring out of the box and said that he wanted me to have it before we met the family so we could tell them all at the same time.

Yes, at last, my prayers were answered. I found my true love and the HUSBAND HUNT was over. What a wonderful Fourth of July this was going to be, fireworks and all. Everyone was so happy for us. My ring was beautiful and I was so excited. This was the start of all our great plans, which we knew could not be put into action until we saved some money for our wedding. Bob knew that we would have to pay for our own wedding. His mother was a widow and had no money to give us. My father did not offer any help either. Bob was working at Bethlehem Steel at this time so he had a good job. We wanted a nice wedding and honeymoon at the shore so we knew we would have to save at least a year to accomplish this. We wanted a summer wedding. It took awhile to put all these plans into action. Even our friends wanted to help with what they could. I only worked as a waitress in a diner so I didn't make a lot of money. We planned a small list of attendees as we were on a tight budget. We finally set our date for

August 22, 1959. Meanwhile, we planned a trip home to Massachusetts to meet my family. I really wanted to show off the "love of my life."

We also wanted to visit Cape Cod as Bob had never been there. So many things to do! As time passed, we discussed who would be in the wedding and all the many details that had to be decided. There were also some fun things to do in planning a wedding. We saw each other as much as we could. Our emotions were running high and sometimes it got the best of us.

Little by little I got to know the family better. We also had meetings at the church on "married life and what we would be encountering," also just what it meant to receive the sacrament of marriage. We had to go for three weeks. We had talks with Fr. Dooley, who was going to marry us, he was a young priest so it was easy to talk to him. He did a good job. I wanted my wedding gown to be made by a dressmaker as I could not find one I liked.

I called my father to find out if he was coming, he said that he would and also my two sisters and my grandmother. They would have to get a room at a hotel for one night. We had a small wedding but a good one with a lot of help from family and friends. In those days, you had friends doing the cooking at the hall. It was a lot of work but people offered to do this for us. We decorated the hall after the church rehearsal. Many people baked desserts for us.

My wedding day started with a phone call from my family telling me that they got here safe and sound. I would not see them until we were at the church. I got dressed at Bob's sister's house for I was living in an apartment that was very small. Her house also would be good for taking photos. We would have a professional picture taken after the wedding, in black and white. The father of one of our friends left us use his Cadillac for our wedding car. It made it special. I had orchids for my bouquet. This was my favorite flower. It was a short ride to the church for we were just a couple of blocks away. We were blessed with so many people to help us have a joyful day. I cried a lot that day for the joy of it. We were happy to know we were loved and blessed by all. At the reception, we had a long Bridal dance and I was very tired by then. We had a full day. I did not have much time to visit my family but I knew they were there for my celebration. It was 11 pm by the time we left the hall. We were ready to call it a day. We were ready to be off by ourselves. We had planned a nice honeymoon in Atlantic City. I had to go back to my apartment and take my wedding dress off to get ready to go away. Our stuff was packed and ready to go. It was 12 am before we got to a motel in Quakertown. We had to find out where the nearest church was as it would be Sunday and we had to go to Mass before we left on our trip. Honeymoon here we come! All the tension of waiting to be alone was finally over. My husband hunt was over. I had found the man of my dreams and now we were starting our new life together. God's great plan was in motion for we were truly blessed with love for each other. We were able to go on our honeymoon with money we received from our wedding. We came home one day early as the money didn't last too long. But we were ready to get settled in our apartment and our new life together. "What God has put together let no man put asunder until death do you part." At this writing, we are together 45 years. Praise the Lord for He is our Leader and Guiding Light. The "power of prayer" is how we have had all these years together.

OUR DAYS OF JOY

✦

(Our First Born)

Robert Richard Amelio Jr. came into this world the hard way after eighteen hours of hard labor. For his Father, it was different. He was bursting with pride that his first born was a boy! It was good to bring him home even though we only had a one bedroom apartment. We had this little space set aside that was only big enough for the crib. We had the crib all set up waiting for the big day to come. Bob had won a big teddy bear which he placed in the crib. When we brought Robbie home I said to the teddy bear. "Move over teddy, the king has come home." Robbie was a wonderful child all his growing years. We loved him so much but had no idea what plans God had for him in his life.

We call him the living miracle because it was the "power of prayers" that encouraged me to take a trip to Lourdes, France. Just me going to France was a miracle in itself, I was asked to go with a person in a wheelchair. She paid for my whole trip. I learned that your prayers are not always answered when you think they should be. My prayers started at the shrine of Our Lady of Lourdes, and many were being said at home. Before I left, my son was having tests done on his back. At this time I did not know that he would get worse after I came home. Robbie was 27 years old when his illness began.

He was a self-employed paint contractor who owned his own business. He needed more benefits for his family so he was trying out for the fireman's test. This included running a mile, which he could not do because of the pain in his back and weakness in his legs. He now realized that something was wrong. After many tests, the doctors diagnosed Robbie with a spinal cord tumor. He had surgery to remove the tumor and then radiation treatments afterwards. Even though the surgery was a success, Robbie was left paralyzed. He has some movement in his legs and full use of his upper body above his mid-section. The road to recovery was not an easy one. Many weeks were spent at the Good Shepherd Hospital working his way back to doing many things on his own. Our blessing is that he learned how to take one day at a time. He has said that his own personal faith and prayer life is what got him through it all. His wife is a strong person and a nurse as well. She helped him to learn to be independent. She gave him her love and support. She also has faith in the power of prayer. I have seen all the wonderful things that he has done for others who are also physically challenged. At first the doctors told him he would never walk again. But God had other plans for him. He used him to be his instrument in dealing with others who have the same problems.

Robbie was always a quiet person when he was growing up but through all this he became a very outgoing person. He can drive and travel on his own with the extra blessings of a modified steering wheel. He has no bitterness regarding the extra efforts he has to deal with everyday. We take these things for granted. One miracle led to another one. He had two daughters before this happened. Katelynn was only nine months old and Trishann was six. He learned to take care of the baby so Pam could go back to work. Rachel was another of those miracles, she was born after his surgery, which was not meant to be. The doctors were amazed; they didn't think this was possible. His surgeon said "this is truly God's work in your life."

Ever since his surgery, he has become more physically active in his community life. He has been employed for four years with the Lehigh Valley Center for Independent Living of Allentown. He is an Accessibility Inspector Plans Examiner. He is coordinator and manager of the Freewheelers basketball team. He speaks to area children, providing awareness about his team. Robbie helped form this team in 1989 so others could be a part of this sport. This helps others build confidence and helps to make them stronger. He gets athletes together and encourages others to go out and get jobs. This is a social network which includes bowling and tennis. His Father told him one time; Amelio's don't ever give up. Robbie has a gift from God helping him find a solution to everyday life. He is outgoing, with a good sense of humor. God gave him a gift to go on and he does it with grace. We are blessed to have a son and his family to share him with. Miracles happen everyday if you just look inside your life you will find them.

God has blessed us with a son who uses the talents given him from the Great Master's Plan to live by. If you open up your heart to the Lord you will have the Master's Plan in your hands to follow. Life is so much easier following his way of life.

MY NEW LIFE WITH THE
HOLY SPIRIT POWER

The everyday stuff happens. This is how I told my story of the ups and downs in my life one day a long time ago. This was before I changed into a spiritually filled person. This is what I shared at our prayer meeting one night. Last Thursday I started my day very badly by arguing with my husband about the children's report cards. This was an awful way to start my day. I tried to do work around the house, but nothing was going right. By lunchtime I could not even see right, I was very upset. I needed to talk to someone, so I stopped in to see my good friend Chris. She asked me to stay for lunch so we could talk. We shared prayer times together and many other things. Chris knew I was not myself. She said, "What is up with you?" I told her about the kid's report cards and our fight about it with BOB and she said her and Tom just did that, also. It did help a little to talk about it, but I still felt sad. I did not like going through this every report card marking period. After leaving Chris' house I started to Praise the Lord but my mood was blue; I felt empty inside. I thought, I am not going to prayer meeting tonight. This was the evil one working on me to keep me from the LORD, and down in the dumps. He did not want me to be with my loving friends. I knew in my heart that I had to go. So much love was waiting for me there. It took me until the next night before I realized that what had happened to me was to have a change in my heart. At the prayer meeting I was praising the LORD in song and sharing with my brothers and sister. I was filling up my cup so I could share with others. The spirit of GOD was renewing me. His wonderful spirit came to us all. Father Lang told us that the LORD fills us up with his love while we praise him so we can go out to give it to others. This is the power of prayer and it is working wherever we go. For we do this in Jesus' name.

ON MY PATH OF LIFE, GOD HAS BEEN MY PRECIOUS ONE

There are many Joys on my "path of life". Yes, I am blessed by God, to be His precious child. All of my life I have followed Him. Each year I have become closer to Him by learning more about Him through the power of prayer. Dear Lord you have opened up many roads for me to walk on. Since I was born, you have been bringing me back to the time, when again, I will be in your loving arms. Each day I start my walk with you, by praying the Rosary and then off to daily Mass to receive food for my soul. This is how I like to start my day. Right now I am walking on my journey of life with Bob, the man that JESUS had put into my life so very long ago. The LORD took me from my home in New England to Florida and then to Pennsylvania so I would meet him. Our journey together has brought us closer than we ever were as young lovers. Years of chaos have made us stronger in our faith. I remember a priest telling me that my job was to lead my husband to God's kingdom. The LORD said "I have put you together to be a loving couple until death due you part, after the crown of glory is placed on your head, then your journey ends. But your life with your heavenly Father will begin." God has blessed us on a journey that started 47 years ago. Jesus has given us many friends and we are truly blessed. We also have a loving family to turn to. We look forward to our resurrection because our KING has told us that he will be there with loving arms. GOD is my life in every passing moment. He is in each person we meet. Sharing time together with a loving family sets us on fire with the love of the HOLY SPIRIT. Sometimes that question comes to mind. What now LORD? Should I be doing more? But someone has to do the praying for others. We can all do that. Mary our Blessed Mother is a gift given to us. She tells her son our needs and he listens to her. This is why he gave her to the whole world. He is our King and she is our Queen forever and ever. This I know for the Bible tells us so. Jesus is the truth, the way, and the light.

(1975) WE ARE CALLED TO WITNESS

We are called to witness by sharing the Lord with others, by asking the Lord to answer our prayers. When we do this, prayer renews us again. We can help others by being our own witness and showing the power of prayer. Jesus gave me a chance at our church bingo one night ...

I was not suppose to work that night but a friend asked me to go in her place. I was very tired from working all day and I was not really up to going, but I went with a heavy heart. Our Lord wanted me there. A good friend of mine, Ida, was there and she asked me to pray with her. She was having trouble at work with her boss. She asked me how to get faith in the Lord like I do. I said by placing your full trust in Jesus and by being faithful with your prayers, that is the only way. As we talked, she shared with me how her boss was giving her a hard time. She felt evil all around her. I told her that maybe the Lord didn't want her there. I also suggested that she pray for her boss to have a change of heart. She said that she never thought of that. She said she would try. She would also pray about whether the Lord wanted her there anymore. She would have to give up her job. So you see if I would have stayed at home I wouldn't have been there to help Ida. I could not have shared my love with her.

Everyday we empty out our love to others. At Mass we pray for the spirit to fill us up by our prayers. In receiving Jesus in our hearts we can give our love again. At prayer meetings I get filled up with his spirit of love again. I did not want to miss out on my filling up of my heart and soul. Only another Christian can give and share this with each other. We understand the ways of the Lord. Jesus fills me with his spirit and love. The Lord wants us to share it wherever we go; anyplace, anytime. When you come to pray with others you get God's love while praising him. We hear God's words each time we are together. When we talk, God is there and so is the love. We asked for his love and he has given it to us in all that we do each day.

A CHARISMATIC PRAYER MEETING

This prayer meeting took place in Atlantic City in (1975) it was on a lecture on the "spirituality of a king who had a banquet." He asked his son to invite the guests. Everyone turned him down. Sometimes Christianity is too good to be true. This is why people don't believe Jesus gave us his spirit to get to know God the Father. When the spirit was given, then and only then could the early Christians pray the "Our Father", who was then called Abba. Jesus spoke to his father. He cried out in the garden. "Take this cup from me." Jesus made us his brothers and sisters so we can call God Abba for He is Our Father. Our whole life in the spirit can be lived by the gifts of the spirit. These are the joys of the spirit: our greatest miracle is that everyone would receive inner peace and our greatest gift is love. So put on your wedding garment from the Lord or you will be turned away from his kingdom. These are some of the thoughts that I received through the most wonderful time I spent on this special Sunday with my prayer friends. The whole day was spent in a spirit of prayer and thanksgiving.

We spent our time catching up on each other's lives during our ride in the car to Atlantic City. We prayed for a safe trip and that we would not get lost. We met up with the "Children of Joy" right away. They had saved us a place for the Mass so we would not have to stand in line. The place was bubbling with smiling faces. A great feeling of excitement goes through you knowing that all these people are here to praise the Lord. The freedom that moves among God's people reminds me of his people being lead by Moses to the "land of plenty". It cannot be put into words how wonderful it feels to be part of Christ's body. One disappointment was that we missed being here on Friday and Saturday. The Masses were beautifully done with love and patience. It was nice knowing that we would also meet up with our old friends from the Acts Group as well as the Children of Joy. It was a powerful experience. The ocean was so beautiful and the boardwalk was filled with God's chosen people. One statement I remember the priest saying is "too bad we have to close this prayerful time but in heaven there are no clocks."

On the way home we shared prayers and also saw the beginning of a large fire in Philadelphia. We prayed that the lives of the people in the fire would be saved. We went by at the right time. The Lord answered our prayers about a safe trip. It turned out that the fire was not as bad as they thought it was. Prayer always comes through. Our time is not the Lord's time. Thank God he does not have a clock in heaven. Praise the Lord for he is good!

WILDWOOD 1976, A VACATION TO REMEMBER ALL TOGETHER

One of our favorite vacations was in 1976 when we went to Wildwood, New Jersey for a week of family fun. We went in September, just before the children went back to school. This was our last trip to the shore as a family. Our children were becoming teenagers and wanted to be with their friends. They were very restless about this vacation. To them this "family stuff" was boring. But somehow we did manage to grow closer together.

This was the first time we had a hotel room with an ocean view. It was almost off-season and many stores were closed. But we didn't care; we were busy enjoying the beach. This was also the first time Diane was forced to be alone with her brothers. This was very different for her. She had to make the most of it for a whole week.

She loved to collect seashells like most people do. This she could share with the boys. Diane wanted to make a special decoration in a jar with everyone putting something into it. It became a family treasure.

David, our youngest, was watching how rough the waves were after a storm. I thought to myself that it must have been that way for Moses when he spread the Red Sea to get away from the evil people chasing them. Our Lord was with them just like the Lord is with us now.

We shared a lot on this trip. Each night we did something different on the boardwalk. Even the air was different than at home. We all love the seashore. Bob got his much needed rest from work. Most important was that we were not rushing here and there. We had time to play games together at our favorite place. We all love to swim so we did a lot of that. Bob helped at bath time so I could have a break too. No dishes to do! We went out every night for dinner.

The week passed all too fast. Before we knew it, we had to say goodbye to the fun at the beach. We took home with us the gift of time spent together which we will all remember in our hearts. Our Lord is so good to us.

WORKING IN JESUS' NAME (1976)

My work was done in his name. I wanted to work after all my children were in school full time so I trained to be a nurse's aid working with older home bound people. I had six cases a day. I worked through the Visiting Nurses Service of Allentown. While doing this job, I gave lots of TLC. I felt at times that the older people were almost like forgotten children who needed to be comforted and told that God did not forget them. He was just making a better place for them. "Why am I still here?" This is a question that was frequently asked of me. They said that they had a good life and were ready to leave this earth. Our Lord has a plan for each of us. It is not for us to say when we are ready to leave. It is His decision.

Many times I could get done with someone in 45 minutes, but I would take time and talk to them and try to comfort them. Whatever they had to say I was the one who would always listen to them. Some had no friends left to tell their stories to. Some of the families were too busy to "hear that story again". Listening was so important to them. After I took care of their needs, I would pray quietly to myself for them. Some people would tell me that they wanted me to come back because I gave them good care. Most aides were in a hurry to get done and be on their way. But I was taking my time because I felt they needed lots of TLC. I knew in my heart I was not just working for the company but in Jesus' name. We did talk about their faith and this made them happy. Being in this kind of work gave me a good feeling about my own needs and purpose in life. I was full of love and our Lord wanted me to pass it on to these people.

When I got home, I still had lots to do with my family so it was double duty. I still had responsibilities at home too. Without God at my side, I could not have been able to do both. This helped me to be on the right track for I knew Jesus was walking with me. While driving to work I would sing His praises so I got my praying done too. Singing is praying twice. I did this kind of work for two and a half years and I learned a lot about health care and myself. When Bob's Mom took sick I was able to be with her and knew what to do to help her. I knew the Lord was with me. I did what I could and it all worked out. This was just one of many jobs I have had over the years. I had to do work that had a purpose, not to just earn money. I knew that God was blessing this work so it meant more to me. I also did a lot of volunteer work as well; some with my own children by my side. We all learned something from the experience.

GOD ASKED ME TO BE HIS VESSEL OF LOVE

On January 29, 1981, Dotty, my dear sister in Christ, was called by the Lord to his kingdom. Before her departure she shared with me that I was given a gift of compassion and understanding of the sick. Dotty and I had met in a prayer group while on retreat at the Villa Maria. The Lord called us together for this parish retreat weekend. Dotty and I were partners. We ended up sharing a lot together. This was part of God's plan for me to do more for my new friend.

Shortly after that weekend, Dotty became very sick with cancer. One of Dotty's fears was what would happen to her beloved husband, Hank after she passed on to be with the Lord. I did not know that the Lord was preparing me to be a part in helping them both through all this suffering. I was asked to be a part of a team to be with Dotty in her last days. Our prayer group formed a visiting chain to be with Dotty when Hank was at work and the nurses were away. Dotty was now in a lot of pain, physically and mentally. She was so grateful to have us visiting her. Hank was happy to know that she was in good hands while he went to work. Her doctor said that we could do more for her than he could. This kind of support was the best for someone with cancer. Just knowing that someone was there helped to shorten the long hours of being alone. Dotty knew that her cancer was progressing. She could feel the love coming from the Girls in the prayer group. When she entered the hospital, I went to visit her there as much as I could. At this time my sister-in-law was also in the hospital. She had had two operations in two weeks. I shared this information with Dotty and she said she would pray for her. Even though Dotty was so sick, she was willing to pray for someone else. My sister-in-law did get better. But Dotty would not.

Each time I went to see Dotty she seemed happier and more peaceful. I had some Holy water, which I put on her from St Ann's Shrine in Canada. A friend had given it to me for my arthritis and now I was sharing it with Dotty. She was getting weak now. She did not know what to talk about but I told her that I loved her and Jesus does too. She was so grateful for the little we could do for her.

I know many people become very fearful when people are near death but God had given me his peace and I was not afraid to be with Dotty at this time. She knew when she woke up that this was going to be the day that the Lord had chosen for her to come to him. She didn't want to talk about it. She was ready to meet her Lord and she was at peace with it. But her husband felt she should talk about it. Both of them knew what was happening. I know her fears were not for herself but for Hank, who she loved so much.

On that last visit I knew the end was near but I still wanted to see her. I had told her that I would be back again. Hank didn't want any company at this time but I said I could just be with her a little bit. She was very weak now and very tired. She recognized me and smiled. I said "do not be afraid, our Lord is with us now". She said," I know." I told her again how much I loved her. I kissed her hand. We prayed the Jesus prayer together. The sun shined on her bed through the window. She smiled and I cried; then I put Holy water on her again. I had a Rosary that was blessed by the Pope, which I put in her hands. We said Alleluia, Jesus loves you and he has a beautiful place for you. She said, "Yes, I know". Then she asked about my sister-in-law. In her time of suffering she was concerned about my sister-in-law whom she had never met. She was a loving person and family was important to her. My hurts were her hurts and that is how it works in God's family. We are united in Christ together. I left Dotty with love and joy in my heart overflowing. She said "goodbye" to me with a smile on her face. Now Dotty was able to let go and was at peace. At the end of the day she did go to our Lord and Hank accepted that she was going to a better place to rest in the arms of Jesus. Praise the Lord!

THE LOVE BIRDS OF 1982

Sometimes you remember being in the same place you were before. This happened on our way to Florida this year. I saw a sign for Beaufort, SC. I started thinking about our trip to pick up Jim from Marine boot Camp. He finally made it. We had taken Evelyn, his girlfriend, with us. She missed him a lot so she asked if she could come with us. He was gone for eight weeks. I remember pulling into this spooky looking town called Beaufort. The moss on the trees at night made it look like Halloween night. It was also foggy so this made it look even scarier. We drove all day and it was now ten pm. We finally got to our hotel. Many other families had come for the graduation so all the hotels were booked. We finally got settled in. We were so tired from the long fourteen hour trip. I could hardly wait to see him the next morning. We were so proud that he finished his training.

Here we were on this military base waiting for the "parade of honors" as it is called. We were allowed to see Jim before everything got started. We were all nervous. We wanted to see him so bad. We had to get up early to get to the reception area. It was a long two months. Jim was the one who always kept us laughing at home but he was also trouble with a capital T. His Father wanted him to get a job right away after he finished school so he wouldn't get in any trouble. Instead he joined the Marines! This was a big step for him. After finding our way to the meeting hall we finally got to see him. I was bursting with tears of joy just to see him again. I wanted to give him a big hug but he explained that "we can't do that at this time." He was being watched and must act reserved. Boy, did Evelyn's face drop with disappointment. He gave each of us a little kiss but we still felt rejected. He was still on duty and this is the way it had to be. He was not the person he used to be. He was so serious. Rules were rules. He did say that he could hardly wait for this to be over. When he got off of base he would let his hair down. He belongs to the Marines now. I was so disappointed that I could not show my feelings. I missed him so much. Then I realized that my son was no longer a boy; he was now a man in the United States Marine Corp! He had to leave to get ready for the parade. We had a cold "Hello" but he had to do what he had to do.

While they were getting ready, we were shown around the base and told how hard a course it is and that not everyone makes it. The ones who do are proud of a job well done. It was great to see all the men marching and hear the band playing. All the families were watching with pride. After the celebration was over Jim had to go back to his barracks to get his bags packed so we got to see where he was staying. His sergeant was passing by and told us that we should be very proud of Jim, as he did a good job in his training. He also said we have a good son. He passed with flying colors. He also said he could tell by working with Jim that he had a good upbringing and a good home-life with caring parents. He shook hands with us and told us that Jim was lucky to have such caring parents. A lot don't. This was a surprise to us as we did not think Jim had it in him to get that kind of notice. This commander thought a lot of Jim and his efforts. This made us feel good too. He has reached his first goal in his life. This was just the beginning of three years of Marine life. He was now able to leave with us but he had to report to his new base in North Carolina in two weeks for more training.

Evelyn didn't like being away from him but this is his job now, so he must go where the service sends him. When we got to the hotel he gave me a big hug and a kiss. He could now relax and be himself. Evelyn felt better too, seeing him relax. They were so much in love, you could see it in their eyes. We knew they wanted to be alone but we were there to make sure that nothing happened. She was only his girlfriend at this point. We were all in the same room so this is the way it was. It was good to talk with Jim in the car on the way home. Jim helped with the driving and we had a good trip home.

Jim was making plans to get engaged to Evelyn but her parents wanted her to go to college and Jim was in the Marines. Evelyn had other ideas. She wanted to marry Jim. She didn't want him leaving again. Soon it was time to go back to base. Evelyn was set on following him to the base and she did just that. Her parents were very upset, as were we. She was a very strong minded girl. Plus, I am sure that Jim wanted her there too. They didn't want to be apart. They decided to get married on his next leave. We didn't agree with this. We felt they were too young and hoped to change their minds. Jim said he had talked to the chaplain on base and that he was counseling them. He was giving them marriage basics. We called our Pastor hoping he would persuade them to wait but that didn't happen either. He talked to them and knowing them all their lives he felt they were ready to be married.

They didn't have any money to have a big wedding, not even a simple one. Her parents knew she had made up her mind so they backed her up. Now it was time to meet Evelyn's parents to discuss the wedding. Before we knew it all the plans were underway. The funny part of all this was that Jim and Evelyn used to play with each other as little children while we mothers were holding girl scout meetings. They were only five years old then. They met again in high school and now here they were getting married. They had gone to the Senior Prom together and had been dating every since.

Jim got leave before Christmas so he planned the wedding then. He was planning on taking his bride back to camp with him. They had an evening wedding and a small reception at her mother's house. They had no money so they could not go on a honeymoon. Going back to camp was the honeymoon.

Well, the marriage lasted five years with many ups and downs but they finally broke up. They had a son who was three when they broke up. It was sad but they both had other interests. Both are married again so we will see how all this works out some day in the future. We are all in God's hands. This I trust and always will.

OUR CHRISTMAS, 1985—OUR SONS WERE AWAY

Christmas was real nice except Jim could not get home from the service. He was stationed in North Carolina and due to be discharged in January 1986. David was also in the service stationed in Germany. He didn't make it home either. I did get a newsletter yesterday, which was great. Bob and I went to 9 am Mass where we greeted many of our friends also celebrating Christ's birthday. This year Bob put up the Christmas tree by himself. I was busy in the kitchen. He did a great job. Usually, he only puts the lights on and I do the rest. But this year he did it all. Not everything is always the same. That is what is nice about changes in life. We had a nice dinner, which started with shrimp cocktail made by Diane. John and Diane were going to serve us as they would be having dinner at John's uncle's house. We had a sixteen pound ham with sweet potatoes and corn and fresh rolls from the oven. A poinsettia plant was our centerpiece. We prayed for Jim and David. We missed them not being with us. We know they were with us in spirit. I had their service photos on the table nearby to remind us of them.

We did have Rudy and Dottie with us for dinner to help fill the void of the missing boys. We opened our gifts before dinner. Trish Ann was happy and talking a lot. Bob Sr. was telling stories at the end of the day. Uncle Rudy, Bob Jr. and Bob Sr. let us to go to the hospital to see Aunt Sophie, who has been very sick and could not be home for Christmas. We talked to Jim on the phone. He was happy to be coming home in January. Everyone wished him a Merry Christmas. We will exchange gifts when they get home.

Last night Aunt Rose and Terri came, with her Christopher, to see our tree. We exchanged gifts with them since we would not see Terri on Christmas Day. She always gives different types of gifts. This year she gave me a Date Book for daily writing and also tea bags with bible sayings on the tags. She gave Bob a puzzle and a folding table to work off of. Bob loves to put puzzles together. We ended up going to their house for holiday drinks and goodies.

We gave Geno a new scarf and a warm sweater. I also gave him a painting of "The Old Man of the Sea", which I knew he would like. I purchased it when I was visiting my sister in New Hampshire.

Our grandchild is due in January. So in 1986 we will have a new little one about for added joy. Children add to the excitement of the holidays. We also have Bob's birthday to look forward to. His birthday is on New Years Eve. We will be at Rudy's house for a party. Bob always gets to be at a party for his birthday. Praise the Lord for all these blessings. It is Jesus' birthday and we get to have fun.

FIRST WE ARE ONE WITH EACH OTHER IN JESUS' NAME

On April 24, 1986 our prayer group planned a special retreat. We were going to Dotty's summer home. One of my Sister's in Christ told me to take notes on this retreat because it would be something special to remember for a long time to come. These notes were also made for those who could not be with us at this time. The Lord had great plans for us. Just getting ready was something else!

First, Ann Lynn forgot her keys in her door so we had to go back and get them. We were already on our way to pick Irene up. Then she realized she forgot her purse at home. She called her daughter to bring it to her. She kept saying that she didn't believe that she did that. Then, as she was closing the car door she spilled soda all over the car floor. This was before we even got on the road! After getting reorganized at Dotty's house and into the car we said a prayer for a safe trip. We were a half an hour late getting started on our trip. Our song to the Lord was "Onward Christian Soldiers" as we drove down route 29 out of town. Ruth was driving and we were sharing stories about our families when a loud blast came down towards us. We looked up and there was a crop duster airplane over our heads. It actually brushed the top of our car! Irene wasn't aware of what had just happened so she just kept talking so we rolled right along. We reached Dotty's place just in time to see a beautiful sunset without anything else happening.

Our Holy Spirit took over the program for our prayer time. It was truly a circle of love. We had breakfast at the house but our other meals would be eaten out so we could relax and have more time to be with each other and the Lord. It was good to see the growth of our love for each other in Jesus' name. Our friendships remain strong over the many years we have been Sister's in Christ together. We just let the spirit flow through us all. It has been eleven years that we have been praying and sharing together.

Walks were always part of our free time but the Lord was always right there with us showing the beauty of his woods and the shore area. On this particular day, Mary Kay started picking wild flowers to make a centerpiece for our table. While walking, we found an old church in the woods where people had a Christian camp set up. This was their prayer space. We were welcomed by two women cleaning the chapel in the woods. They showed us a wooden cross that has been there for many years. It was made by children, who were there before. It was made of sticks found in the woods. We were invited to come back any time to pray. It was wonderful to share prayers with these other Christians. An added bonus was the beautiful weather we were having. It was nice and sunny all weekend. After our noon prayer time we headed to town for shopping. We enjoyed lunch at a Scandinavian gift shop. They had some really neat things which came from Sweden. Dotty and I even ended up with the same bathing suit. That was funny! We had a great time shopping together.

We attended mass Saturday evening. The priest gave a powerful message reminding us that we were all in God's hands. The restaurant that we ate dinner at had flowers all around. It was like being in a garden. Irene was our camera lady taking photos all weekend. She wanted to get everyone's picture.

At nighttime, our prayers were healing and uplifting. Then there was the bathroom. Who would believe that seven women could share one bath? And no fighting either!

We were truly children of God sitting at the table of the Lord. The Holy Spirit was teaching us a lot. Dotty always had a dream of having a prayer meeting at her and Art's hide-away place on the Delaware. Now this has happened. It was so nice of her to have us there. We were so happy to be there. The walks by the ocean were so beautiful with the sun on our faces in the day and the moon and stars at night. We are blessed with many gifts of nature. We gave him our praise and our love. Our hearts and souls were lifted up to him. We have an awesome God. He is so good to us all. We will all remember this encounter with Jesus and each other. We have shared many retreats but none like this one. A TV and radio was available but we did not want or need them. We were happy to just be in the presence of the Lord. We did not know what the rest of the world was doing but we knew that we had a little bit of heaven where we were. We had Jesus with us and we had each other.

One of the last readings from the Bible was: If God is for you, who can be against you? We have to trust and know that Jesus walks with us. Songs on the tapes helped us relax and get into prayer easily. We really didn't want to leave but like all good things they have to come to an end. On the way home Ruth needed to stop for gas. Dotty was in the lead car so we had to get her attention by honking the horn. But she didn't hear us so Irene put up a sign as we passed them to: PLEASE STOP. She finally got the message. We were flying on Angel's wings. That's for sure. The whole trip home was filled with laughter and joy. Funny little jokes were popping up here and there. One thing we know is that over all the years our friendship has grown because we have put the Lord first in all we do with each other. Our Lord has a Master Plan and we do it together. He has put us together for a reason. We are his body with his circle of love and it keeps going round and round for Jesus and us. No one can keep us apart even into eternity.

LIFE IS NOT ALWAYS A BED OF ROSES

"Life is not always a bed of roses." The year 1986 will always be marked in my book as the year of many changes in our so-called routine of family life. It was "far from routine" the morning I received the call from an Air Force man telling me that our son David had a bad car accident in Wiesbaden, Germany. He was being treated at the medical center there. We were very upset to say the least. The man from the Air Force asked us how soon we could be ready to leave for Germany to be with our son. He knew that this was very hard on me but he was very understanding to wait for me to get under control. I told him that I would call him back as soon as I could figure out what I needed to do and get it done.

It seemed like we had just seen him off at the airport to go to Germany for his duty, which he was so excited about. At this point I could only think about who I should call first. I called my best friend, Rose, and her daughter, Terri, for they would be able to help me the fastest. Next I called my daughter, Diane. She could handle the arrangements that had to be made with the military. By now I could hardly talk. Diane called her dad and he came home immediately to be with me. Many things had to be done. Diane made all the arrangements for our trip. The Air Force wanted us to leave on Saturday. This was going to be an emergency flight. The Air Force was trying to make everything run smoothly for us. The State Department had to get us papers so we could leave the country without a passport. Everything had to be worked up quickly. It was hard to make decisions with a heavy heart and not knowing how David was. Would we get there in time? How is he? These are the questions that were running through our minds.

We had to pack but we weren't sure what to take. We were going somewhere that we didn't know what the weather would be like. We also didn't know how long we would be there. Everyone was so concerned and offered their help. We called my prayer group so they would know what was going on and offer their prayers. We knew that prayer support was most important.

Additional stress was added when our daughter-in-law had a small car accident on her way home to be with us. Then our son-in-law hurt his eyes at work which added more stress; all these things happening on the same day. Our friends Rose and Eugene said they would take us to New York for our flight. That was one less thing to worry about. At this time I was running Grandma's Play Room. We had to call all the parents and have them pick up their children and make other arrangements for them.

Everything was arranged by the Air Force for our flight out of the US. In New York we met with army personnel to help us with all the paper work.

She also let us know what would be happening with these last minute plans.

Her job was to see that we were made comfortable and that we got on the plane. Thanks to all our family and friends, things were moving along. Our friends waited until we were on the plane before they left for home in case there was a change of plans. Bob also had to get a leave of absence from his job. His boss was very understanding and said to take whatever time he needed. He knew that Dave was in serious condition. There were so many details to take care of and all under stress.

It was late afternoon when we finally got on the plane. It was a good trip as the plane was one of the big planes that go to Europe all the time. Dinner was served and then a movie was shown but I fell asleep during that. The next time I woke up it was with the sun coming through the window. It was morning and we were landing after eight hours of flying. We were finally in Germany. We had never been on a plane this long. We did not rest well for our minds and hearts were on what was happening with David. We were taken to customs where two Air Force men were waiting for us holding a sign saying AMELIO and we knew it was for us. We were taken to a special room. The military men had to talk the German officers into letting us into the country without a passport. They explained that this was an emergency trip to see our son. All we had was our birth certificates. They were not happy about that. But they left us in. They stamped our papers and we were on our way. Everywhere we went we had to show these papers. Security was pretty high at this time. It gave us a strange feeling.

The men from the Air Force helped us with the suit cases. They took us to a waiting car. We were taken to the hotel where we would be staying which was right next to the hospital where Dave was. We just dropped our suitcases off at the hotel and hastened to the hospital as we wanted to see Dave right away. When we got to the hospital the doctor explained what Dave had been going through. Everyone was alerted to our coming. I will not forget the welcome that the doctors and nurses gave us. The Doctor told us that just being there would give Dave a reason to live. He was in a lot of pain and he had all kinds of tubes hanging everywhere from his body. When we first saw him he said he thought he was going to die. He was under a lot of medication and then could not talk as he would fall asleep. The doctor said this was good as he needed his rest. At one point Dave opened his eyes and he saw us. We let him know that we were there for him. He was afraid to close his eyes thinking that he would not wake up. He was hurt more than we realized. Dave was first taken to a small emergency place after the accident. They thought he only had a broken leg but soon found out that there was more to it. It was to be a long road back to recovery. Meanwhile, we found out that the men who picked us up at the airport turned out to be a Major and a Sergeant from Dave's unit. Once Dave saw us he didn't want us to leave. We were so tired from our trip but we reassured him that we would be back in the morning. The doctor told us that he had a collapsed, bleeding lung. It was so hard to see all of this happening. I went to the chapel to pray by myself.

The hotel where we were staying was called the Amelia Earhart Hotel. This was a military place for people with emergency cases. It only cost us $36 a day. This helped a lot. I prayed for David to have the bleeding stopped so he could breathe better and get well again. The catholic chaplain was off for the weekend. David had not received the "anointing of the sick".

I was told to call Susan, from the Red Cross, if we needed anything. I called her about this matter and she said that she would see what she could do about getting us a priest to anoint David. What wonderful people GOD puts into your life wherever you are. I knew that everyone at home was praying for us all so many miles from home. You could feel the power of prayer.

The night before, a priest came from town. He was German and could not speak English very well but he prayed over David and reassured us that he received the blessing of the sick. I did not care what he talked like; I just wanted David to have this given to him. The next day being Sunday, we went to Mass at the chapel in the hospital. The catholic chaplain was to return by then. After Mass was over he came to us and said that he was sorry that he was not here when we came in. He offered to help in any way that he could so I made an appointment with him for the next morning. I had so many questions on my mind. He knew the danger that Dave was in. We were at Dave's bedside as much as we could be. We only left to eat, to keep up our strength. I was on a small nerve pill which my family doctor had ordered before I left home. This was so stressful for both Bob and I. Bob was getting headaches but would only take aspirin for them. He told David that he didn't come all these miles to see him die so he better get well.

On Monday morning, Susan, from the Red Cross, called to see if there was anything she could do for us and wanted to know if everything was alright with where we were staying. She would like to meet with us soon to answer any questions that we might have. I said that we would soon make a time to be away from David but he was not out of danger yet. Also, an officer from Family Affairs called to get Dave's personal things taken care of. She was to call General Peabody today to look into the fact that David had an apartment and a car to take care of. She would have to do all these things for him for he would not be able to take care of this stuff for a long time. Another woman came from the Red Cross to offer the use of her home phone for our calls to the states. We could do that tomorrow.

One of the calls that we received was from someone in the Air Force named Alice Bagly. She came from a place called Lindsey Station, around the corner from the hospital. She told us that we would have to get a temporary pass to get in and out of the hospital and hotel. We would have to show the pass. So many details in this place just adding to our stress even though everyone was trying to help.

The report given to us by the doctor was not good news. They realized that David had a lot more wrong with him than just a broken leg. The big problem was that he had bleeding in his chest and his one lung had collapsed. His jaw was broken and he had glass in his face which would require plastic surgery at a later date. The main bone in the middle of his leg was a mess. They couldn't do surgery on it until the bleeding in his chest stopped. One thing at a time! The other people that were in the accident were recovering and out of the hospital already. He was the one who was thrown out of the car and into a tree. So his condition was the worst. Everything was being done that could be at this point. This is why the Air Force flew us over here so that we would be here for Dave's support and give him the will to live. I again prayed in front of the Blessed Sacrament asking the Lord to save my son. We needed a miracle and I was not afraid to ask the Lord for it. It was in His hands. At night we would leave the hospital after Dave was asleep. Then we would go for dinner. We were not really hungry but knew that we had to keep our strength up. Then it was back to the hotel to try to rest.

Here we are in this strange country. Bob was so funny. He saw a little store nearby as we were going for a walk. It said Minn Mall. I guess it was like a Seven Eleven. He was trying to shop like he did at home. He was so funny for we only had one piece of German money and the cashier did not speak English. So we said "what can we buy for this one bill?" I was so upset because he had all these little goodies like he buys at home and not enough money to pay for it. We had so many fights it was unbelievable, with the tension we were under. Well we made it back to the hotel with some of the goodies anyhow.

When we went to see Dave in the morning, the doctors said that the bleeding was slowing down. We prayed for it to stop. His lungs were in bad shape. If all goes well, he will have to get surgery on his leg on Friday and then his jaw will have to be wired up. He will not be able to eat solid food for about two weeks. I was hoping he could come home to get better. He did like the nurses and the men who were taking care of him. He was getting top care as there were not many patients there at that time. Dave was starting to put things together about the accident. He was upset because he could not talk. He wrote things on paper but he could hear everything. He was alert by this time. The nurses took the stitches out of his face. The doctor took the stitches out of his leg but he will have to have more surgery on Friday. His lungs started to improve after the tubes were taken out. Then he will be able to talk to us. His girlfriend, Karen Ruff, called from the states. Just hearing her voice lifted his spirits up. I talked to Diane and Rose today. It costs less for them to call us than it would be for us to call from Germany. Phone service is very expensive here. On Friday we have to go and get our passports for we only have temporary papers. This would mean taking a trip to Frankfurt which was about an hour away. We didn't want to leave but we had to do this, as we didn't know how long we would be here. Dave was having surgery today and we wouldn't see him very much anyway.

September 30, 1986

Dave is starting to look better but he had to have two blood transfusions today. This made him even more depressed today. They told him that his jaw had to be wired so it could mend. Also, some of his teeth were loose. He also thought that when they took the tubes out he would be able to talk but this was not going to happen because of the surgery on his jaw. He knew what was happening but he was angry because he still had to write everything on paper. One step at a time! We all have been dealing with so many emotions.

We will be going with Shelley, from the Red Cross, to make phone calls because the phone systems were not good here. We stayed with Dave until 1:00 am last night. He has good people working with him. He asked the nurse when he would be able to leave and she said in about two months.

A minister, named Greg Carlson, came and prayed with us. He was very nice and we found him to be a comfort to us. Our days were spent by Dave's bedside. He was very tired at times, so when he rested, I would write post cards. Bob worked on his number word books. We were hoping that the lung tube would be taken out soon. We did leave the hospital to go for dinner and to freshen up. We got some more things at the drug store. I made pictures of the family on paper while Dave was sleeping so he would see familiar faces. The whole staff really worked hard to keep him going. We were getting adjusted to the hotel and the food. Everything has been good, or should I say as good as it could be in a strange place thousands of miles away from our home and family. Our mission was to help Dave.

Aunt Rose called again. It helps to know that so many of our family and friends are concerned and praying for us. It was another beautiful day today. Dave is getting his legs and arms worked on to keep his blood flowing so he will not get stiff. He had the oral surgeon talk to him about putting the wires in so his jaw can mend. Another bone surgeon will repair his leg. It is good that the hospital is right next to our hotel. All we have to do is walk across the court to the hospital.

TV here consists of one English Channel and is run by the American Air Force. The staff all wear their uniforms. This seems funny to us. Dave told Dad how the Eagles won their game on Sunday, which was old news, but he knew he would like to know that. Dave is on a lot of pain medication. The Caulfield's called us the first night we were here, as well as Aunt Rose and Diane. It is good to hear their voices wanting to know how we are doing.

Everybody is keeping in touch. I was supposed to do some calling with a person from the Red Cross but we did not get that connection yet. GOD is so good to us for letting us know that we are blessed with good friends.

October 1986

We are now in the month of October. Today I got up at 6 am so I would have time to praise the LORD before our busy day started. At 7 am I heard the church bells ringing from our hotel room and I wondered where they were. I looked out the window and I could see two church steeples but someone had said that it was far away. I could see that there were crosses on top so I wanted to find out if it was a Catholic Church. I woke Bob up at 8 am so we could go to breakfast. It was another sunny day. We were at the hospital by 9:30. The nurses were working on him so we went down stairs to wait. I decided to go to the chapel to pray. Dave has a great fear of death. Bob has been helping a lot with Dave. This seemed to be a man to man time for them. Our emotions were all running high. I knew that JESUS was with him but it was hard to get a catholic priest to say prayers for Dave. I really thought that these spiritual things would be automatically taken care of in the military but I wonder now. The catholic chaplain was still on leave but I thought they would have someone to take his place. The minister was there but I wanted him anointed by a catholic priest.

A physical therapist will be working with him. He has so much to be done. Last night we saw his leg being dressed. It was not a pretty sight. He is being well taken care of. Some more calls from home. Aunt Rose and Uncle Geno and James called.

October 2, 1986

Well, the days are moving along. It is now Oct 2nd. We got the news that Dave will not have to go to surgery yet. At last ... a catholic priest came in to anoint Dave. We were so glad to meet him. I prayed in the chapel in the morning and JESUS answered my prayers. Father was so upset that they did not call him right away with his serious condition. He said that he would look into it. Dave has a lot of fears and he is full of questions. The staff has been great to all of us.

Dave's friends, who were in the accident with him, came to see him yesterday. Their visit sure lifted his spirits. He even was joking around on paper. We are getting bits and pieces about the accident. He was only a little way from his apartment when it happened. Dave has a long road ahead of him and so do we. I went to the Red Cross yesterday. They will help us with our hotel bill so we don't have to use up our everyday expense money. Everyone is so helpful. Everything is being done that could possibly be done for us and Dave. So here we are in Germany but not by choice or to have fun. This has been a very stressful time for us. But we are hanging in there.

We did not get up until 10 am today. I was up at 6 am, got a shower, and went back to bed. I went to sleep and had a dream about Uncle Geno. He came for us and we had to hurry because it was going to snow. What a dream! When we got to the hospital we found out that Dave will have to have surgery done on his leg on Friday. Dave was very depressed about everyone telling him different stories. He is very upset. He did not want to talk to me. He wanted to talk to Bob, man to man. His lungs are coming along and he is making progress. I went to pray in the chapel for awhile this afternoon. When I came back from prayer, things seemed to calm down with Dave. It was a nice sunny day so we took a walk for a change of pace. We walked to Lindsey Station to let Alice help us change some of our money to German money. We are going shopping on Saturday, if all goes well with Dave's surgery. One thing we found was that the military works 12 hour shifts. With nursing this is really long and hard.

One of Dave's friends, who was in the accident with him, stopped in to see him. He is in the army and he had to go back to work even though he hurt his shoulder and his arm is still in a sling. I think this is awful. How cruel that they have to go back to work even though they are hurting. But this is the army! The car was totaled. There were two other accidents in the same place.

Dave has round the clock care. He has to have his leg in a cast. It will be a long recovery. We will be here for most of it. The doctor said his bone was outside his leg which made it more dangerous of infection. Dave also has a broken jaw in two places which need to be wired together. Dave is very fearful of all that has to be done. Being in bed is awful in itself. Everyone is doing their jobs but Dave is on a lot of drugs for pain and rest. All his friends want to see him but they are not allowed to be here right now. Dave thought that we would be going home by now. He has so many things to get done that he does not want to be alone. He really wants us here. We will be here for him. We must do a lot of praying that all this will go well.

Dave was so depressed because he thought we were going home. The surgeon was in to see him and told him what had to be done to get him back on his feet. He still thinks he's going to die. It is not easy to understand all of this stuff that is being done. One thing we found out is that young people don't share with their chaplain because of respect of their rank.

Oct 3, 1986.

I woke up at 4:55 am so I started my prayers. I said my Rosary and then took my shower and got ready to see Dave, knowing that he was going for surgery today. He had a good night and was well rested. He was now looking forward to getting his leg worked on so he could get out of bed. We also had to go with SG Ferguson to get our passports done. It would mean going to Frankfort. Frankfort is protected by all kinds of security, electric gates, and barriers. We had the VIP treatment all the way. It took us 45 minutes just to get there. Now back to the hospital to see how our son made out. All the staff could hardly wait to see our faces when we came in to see Dave. He was a different person. He had a cast on his leg but was happy the surgery was over for now. Everyone was happy for us.

We went to the Red Cross to apply for a grant to pay our hotel bill due to the fact that our Master Charge bill was piling up with high interest. Also, the German money is down in value. When we got back Dave was sitting in a chair falling asleep. By then we were falling asleep too. It was a long day. So we left to go to dinner. We did have good meals. Then back to the hospital to see Dave. He was so much better even though he had an oxygen mask on. He could finally talk to us. We told him that we had to go back to the hotel to receive a call from the kids.

One of the nurses is taking us shopping down town to show us around, as she has the day off. This will be a much needed break from our routine. We met Fr. Walsh today, he is back from leave. He said he was sorry that he was not there for us in our time of need. He did not know why his substitute was not called in. He is so free flowing and jokes around with us. Dave really likes him too. He was sleeping when we visited with him. If all goes well, he will be moved to a regular room today. The weather here has been great, so far. We saw all the hospital staff in their uniforms today because they had to go on field duty right outside of the hospital. A helicopter was the study of the day with injured people. It was just a test. The Air Force has been so helpful. We have been dealing with nurses who are captains and all kinds of top ranking people. It is an experience I will never forget plus the good work they have been doing with Dave. Praise the Lord for answering our many prayers. We finally got our passports fixed. It is easier to get by now, due to the high security everywhere.

Oct 4, 1986

Today is my birthday. We started out early so we could visit with Dave early. We planned to go down town to tour a little bit, just to get away from the hotel and the hospital. The sun has been out everyday that we have been here. Our new friend, Amy Richardson, who was one of Dave's techs, has offered to show us around. She was so helpful, such a nice person. I was very interested in the beauty of the homes and buildings. We started by looking at clothing which was very expensive. I was looking for a night gown and also got a pair of sneakers. It was good that I got them as we walked everywhere. It was so different, so many people in the street with their baskets over their arms to carry their things home. In Germany, a woman shops every day for her food so everything is fresh. We learned that in Germany the main meal is at noon time. Everyone comes home from work for two hours to have their meal and then they go back to work. All the stores close also until four in the afternoon. We stopped at Burger King for lunch. Just like at home but the signs were in German. Bob was hot so he went across the street for a beer and a German sausage sandwich. So Amy and I talked over lunch. While having lunch, we heard a band playing in the street. There were many stores with bakeries, plus shoe stores, clothing stores, and jewelry and perfume shops. The antiques were neat but very expensive. Each one was different and the buildings were so interesting. We climbed up a hill to find our way to a place called the Dome. It was really a sight to see. It was a Russian Church monument made for a princess who died there. The top of the Dome was made of solid gold. We walked up many hills but then we took a trolley ride to the princess's resting place. From this high place we could see the whole city of Wiesbaden. You could actually see the smog being produced from so many cars. The parks are well kept, flowers everywhere. To see a real neat view we went to a cafe' on the top of this mountain. We sat outside to have coffee and tea, Bob a beer. The trees were so tall. Saturday is a day to be with family so the parks were crowded with many children. Such a nice place to play. The parks were filled with roses. The windows in the homes have beautiful lace curtains. I took pictures of things along the way. Amy said she would like to live in one of these big beautiful homes. We went into a Russian Church which had all kinds of art work everywhere. I bought post cards of this place for it would be something to show everyone at home. I was enjoying the sights but I also wanted to get back to Dave. It was a good day for my birthday, even though I missed being home with family. A big party was planned for me at home before all this happened but it got canceled and I never did have another one like they were planning. The Lord had a different plan for us which we soon came to find out.

Oct 5, 1986

I woke up at 6 am and took a nice hot shower. Praise the Lord for this new day. I got Bob up for Sunday Mass. Fr. Walsh said a beautiful Mass today. He is surely filled with the Spirit. He shared the Spirit on "how each day should be an important day for us because no one knows how many days we have to enjoy God's beautiful world before he calls us to himself. Count your blessings each day and your gifts that God has given to you." We had a lady Eucharistic Minister serve us the Lord's blood and Fr. gave us His body. It was a very nice Mass in the hospital chapel. We went back to the hotel for breakfast. I enjoyed the grits which reminded me of home. It was a beautiful day, again. Dave was sleeping when we went to visit with him, so we left to go and relax, for yesterday was a very busy day. But I ended up doing laundry before I went to bed. James called me to wish me a Happy Birthday. Rose also called and my son Bob; I missed the calls as I was doing the wash. I will have to wait for another day to talk to them. Dave is doing well today. Fr. Walsh stopped in to see Dave and he talked with all of us. He is the type who likes to joke around. I am praying he will be able to help Dave get back to church with praising the Lord to have more meaning in his life.

Oct 6, 1986

I was very upset today. I woke up at 4:30 and I started to pray because I could not sleep. So I started to think about what to do about Dave's future after he gets back to the states and out of the service. I was feeling depressed and crying at the drop of a hat. Dave was doing better today. He is also starting to eat better. He will be moving up to the third floor soon. We had a meeting with the oral surgeon and he explained about the wiring of his jaw and how it would be all wired together until it healed. Captain Hanson realized I was having a problem, she could tell I was sad today. She helped me understand how far Dave had come. She also remarked on how much progress he had made in such a short time. Praise God. I made an appointment with Fr. Walsh for he could help me for he was full of the Spirit. He is a man well suited for his job. My talk with him helped me understand the military ways.

A lawyer came to talk to Dave so he can get his bills paid by selling his car. Other things at his apartment will have to be taken care of as he will not be able to do all these things for awhile. He will have to go back to living on base. He will not be able to drive for a long time. A young lady came to help him get his personal matters taken care of. I talked to Fr. Walsh and he helped me get a lot of my feelings out with all that has been happening. I had a lot of crying to let out for I had been holding that all inside. I was really homesick and I wanted to be at home. But I also wanted to be here for Dave. Captain Hanson also helped me get over my depressed feeling by answering my questions. We finally got back to the hotel for dinner. After dinner we went for a walk. We found a curtain store. It was very different from our stores at home. I had heard about the curtains from a German woman that I knew from our church at home. She told me all about how beautiful the lace once was. We are getting adjusted to getting around here now.

Dave is now getting physical therapy. He has so many doctors that are helping him it is hard to keep up with them all. We started our day late today. It was 11 am before we went over to see Dave. He is busy with so many things in the mornings now. He now has a TV to watch. Bob is also pushing him around in a wheel chair. Everyday he is making progress. One day at a time. At night I am so tired that I can hardly write things of the day. Diane called today. It was good to hear her voice.

Oct 7, 1986

I did not sleep good last night. Dave was sleeping when we got to the hospital. We also had a small problem. I had lost the hotel key. We had a treasure hunt in the room before we left. I was praying to St Anthony to help us find it. Here I am in a dark room looking for the key. I emptied my purse twice. Then I went to the suitcase and emptied it twice. I looked on the floor, everywhere I could think of. It will cost us $10 to replace the key. I knew that Bob would be mad at me. He was very upset. Next I took the bed apart. Just another thing to add fuel to the fire. This we did not need now. Bob left to get coffee, as he was so angry. By the time he came back St Anthony had answered my prayers. We found the key. I don't remember where it was. I was just glad to find it.

I went to the chapel to praise and thank the Lord for the blessing of Dave's progress. He got moved upstairs today so he has to adjust to a new room and also his room mate. He took one look at his room mate and said "I am in good shape compared to him". This man was in a car accident too but he had more things wrong with him than Dave. Bob and Dave had fun going up and down the hallways with the wheelchair. By the time he got settled in his room we were tired so we left to get some rest. Fr. Walsh offered to take us for a ride along the Rhine River to see the castles. We may do that.

We are projecting going home next week. Dave gets his jaw wired and fixed on Wednesday which won't be comfortable at all. But it has to be done. He is on a lot of medication for infections and pain. This will all help to heal his leg wounds. We are hoping that there will not be any complications. This going back and forth to the hospital every day is getting us down. But, that is what we are here for. A lawyer has been helping Dave's personal affairs get taken care of. Dave has a friend who is willing to help him sell his car and give up his apartment. Karol is going to take us to Hahn base so we can see Dave's apartment. She will be off on Thursday so we'll do it then. I had a bad day yesterday. It finally all hit me about what has happened here. I talked to Captain Hansen, the head nurse, who helped Dave when he first came to the ICU unit. She explained a lot of what was happening with him. It helped me understand more of all that is being done for him. I also made an appointment with Fr. Walsh to talk about my blue feelings. He said I was suffering from homesickness. It also hit me that we could have lost our son. Praise the Lord for putting Fr. Walsh into our life. I know that there was a lot of praying going on at home too. We are trying to prepare Dave for the time when we have to go home. It will be hard on us all. We must go home soon.

The nurses on the new floor seem to be really nice. Rules on this floor are tough. It was a cloudy day today but this is the way it is here this time of year. When we got to the hospital Dave was still sleeping so we went for a cup of tea. The staff on the ICU floor said good bye to him before he went up to the new floor. They were all so nice to him. They worked well together. Thanks to them he was able to move on with his treatments. Dave had to say goodbye to Amy, the nurse helper, who seemed close to his age. She seemed crabby today. Maybe she doesn't like goodbyes. I got a book on Hummels today because we are hoping to get one for Diane before we go home. We had a nice dinner downstairs and

Bob is watching a football game. We can only get one USA TV station. So what you see is what you get. Dave is starting to push his own wheel chair around now. This is a good sign. The Red Cross has offered to help us with our hotel bill with a grant; meaning we don't have to pay it back. This is to help us so we can have enough cash for the rest of the time that we are here. We are waiting to see what the doctors say about Dave's recovery. He gets 30 days state side because he was injured while on duty. When he is in traveling condition he will be able to come home. We just have to wait. A lot of paper work has to be done. We were so blessed to be so near to the hospital. In Hitler's days, during the Second World War, this hospital was his, the hotel was his headquarters. What a landmark we are at. This hotel is called Amelia Earhart's Hotel. The club part and the food part belong to the military. The hotel itself belongs to a private hotel service. On the floors are the German signs of Hitler. Down in the basements there are still secret tunnels that they had during war times. This is for the military and their families. It is so interesting how all this works. Lindsey Air Force station is around the corner and that is full of history too. We took a walk last night and we saw different stores. A place across the street is a fast food place with German sausage and stuff. One blessing after another has come our way so Praise the Lord. Before we left home our good friends from my prayer group came to comfort us. Dotty Trexler and Mary K. were right there with us. It is good to know that we have many good people to back us up at a time like this. They offered us money and prayers; whatever they could do to help. We are thankful for all that was done for us at that time.

Oct 8, 1986

It is cloudy today and it is hard to believe that we are on a big hill but you can hardly see anything of the city. Today Dave is having his bone surgery and his jaw wired. We will see him before he goes in for surgery. I did wake up early so I said my Rosary. I will get to Mass today at 11:30. Dave is returning to the same floor but he is returning with a back full of pain. While Dave was in surgery, we went to have tea. Then we went to Mass with Fr. Walsh but he was called away on an emergency, so we just ended up receiving the Eucharist. We took a walk and looked at the churches which we could see from our hotel. They were a beautiful sight to see. From the outside it was neat but the doors were locked so we could not get inside. So we walked down the hill where we found a neat bakery. There were all kinds of goodies to pick from. It was good to walk somewhere different. We did not walk long for we were too concerned with what was happening with Dave. When we got back, he was in a bad mood so we didn't stay long.

I stopped in to see Shelley Carter, from the Red Cross; she told us some things that would help us when we were ready to go home next week. We wanted to see how Dave was doing with everything first. Bob has been doing everything for Dave; he does not want me anymore. It has become a man to man thing. I do feel rejected at this point. I am trying to understand this turn-about. Now it is Bob's turn to care for Dave. Dave thinks that he will be in bed for days. His emotions are up and down right now. My foot is hurting a lot from the walk this morning. Dave got a lot of mail today.

Oct 9, 1986

We had a nice dinner last night even though my foot was bothering me again. We went to see Dave but he was not in a good mood. He gets angry when I try to help him. It's hard to make him realize that we are here to help him. Does he want us to go away? I wish I knew because I am hurting inside for him. My feelings get all mixed up when we talk about going home. Dave just started on liquid food. He gets such pain in his leg that tears come to his eyes. He has a low tolerance for pain, like me, I guess. Bob has been with him a lot so I feel that this is a man to man time again and I am on the outside looking in. I am praying to God for courage to be able to help him. He is off all shots for the pain so he will have to learn to tolerate the pain. I am also praying that he will be able to cope with all of this. Diane called last night at 7:45 her time, we were in bed sleeping. Bob had some wine with dinner so he was relaxed and sleeping away but I woke him to talk to her. Diane and John want to buy a lot to build a house on. She wanted to tell us about it.

Here I am enjoying this nice sunny day in the patient lounge, it is a pretty room with light blue walls. It also has a balcony so patients can go outside to enjoy the sunshine too. The trees are turning colors now. The sun is warm and the roses are still in bloom outside. Flowers are everywhere in the shops and hanging from the balconies. The floor that Dave is on is very busy now. There are 55 patients on Dave's floor so he has to wait his turn. This is an adjustment from ICU where everyone was nearby to help him. But if he is in trouble, they will be there for him. Top matters must be taken care of first and getting out of bed is a treat when you cannot help yourself. It is a humbling experience to depend on others for your needs. I feel helpless right now. We have to go back home next week if everything is going well with Dave. We are supposed to go to Hahn today with a friend of Dave's. So we are waiting for her to come so we can see Dave's base.

Bob has been dealing a lot with Dave and his pain. He gets mad at me. He is dealing with so much right now. He got his jaw wired yesterday and everything seems to be going the way it should. He went to x-ray this afternoon. He is now off the penicillin. He is with men worse off than he is. We spent a lot of time at the hospital today but we have decided that we have to go home next week. We have been here for two and a half weeks now. We would return home on Oct. 15th, all the arrangements have been made. We would be leaving Wednesday on a Mac Flight. It will not be easy to leave Dave for so much has to be done yet for Dave to be on the way to good health. But he is out of danger now. We have the phone number to be able to reach him. I sat in the rocking chair that was in the patient lounge for I miss our chairs at home. I miss everybody from home too. We went to see Alison Bagley from the Lindsey Station to set up our tickets for our airfare home. Pam called us to see how things were going and we cried together. She told us how much she has missed us. We miss them too. Dave's friends came in to see him. They all seem nice. We have been made welcome by all the young people. They all come from different backgrounds. Some of them were from Pa. I met a family from Pittsburgh, who just arrived here.

Oct 10, 1986

I did not sleep well last night due to the Italian meal we had. The meal was good but I was up all night with heartburn. Bob didn't sleep well either. He heard the people next door having a gay old time. Dave didn't sleep well with all the machines beeping on and off. Also his room mate snores a lot. He has so much to cope with these next months it will be difficult. He will need lots of support. He was out of his wheel chair when we arrived this morning. He is not a morning person. I really don't know what to say to him at this time. One tech nurse misunderstood our talks and thought we were fighting. She asked us to stop. It is getting harder and harder not to get into these discussions. It must sound awful to other people. His friends said that they will visit with him after we leave. I hope they don't forget him. Some of the things we were wondering about were; is Dave going to have psychological counseling about the accident? We wanted to talk to his doctors before we leave here. We wanted to know what else had to be done. How would they keep us informed? By the time we tried to set up an appointment with the staff it was a holiday and were away. So this never took place.

Oct 11, 1986

I started my day with the Rosary for October is the month for Mary. I also did my wash. I am waiting for Bob to get ready. He is tired today but we are going to wait to see Dave this afternoon because he is busy with his therapy. He's very crabby in the mornings anyway. He still has a lot of pain. Amy came to see him. She's the nurse from ICU. I think she likes him. She said she would visit with him. Dave gets around in the wheel chair but he gets tired easy. Aunt Rose calls everyday. She sounds like she's just around the corner. I had a talk with Dave because he was so depressed about being in bed with nothing to do. After our talk we got him laughing but it made his jaw and ribs hurt. But we laughed anyway. Bob made a smiley face on Dave's sock so he would not be so crabby in the morning. Dave's friend, Mike, came to see him. He was one of the guys in the accident with him. Then that night Dan and Christine came to see him. After their visit they took us bowling and out for dinner. Dave's friends all seem so nice. We hope they all stick by him when we leave. Praise God for all that He has helped us with. I have been praying that Dave would be able to come state side to finish his recovery at home. He wants out of the Air Force but I don't think this will happen.

We have decided to visit Dave in the afternoon now as he is so crabby in the morning. The nurses have a lot to do for him then too. So we decided to take a walk. We went to an Italian Restaurant called Keller, which in German means cellar. It was in the cellar but it was so beautiful. We had two waiters to bring our food. We had Lambrusco but it tasted like Champagne to me. It was good. Everything was so good and we topped it off with ice cream. Dad had Italian cake. I had my tea served in a fancy glass cup that kept it very hot. It was a nice time. We are doing a lot of walking down the hill. Walking is very hard on our feet and I am having a heel spur problem now. We might go bowling with Dave's friends. We were supposed to go to Hahn but we misunderstood the date. So we might not get there. Dave wanted us to see Hahn. Right now I am feeling very rejected by Dave's attitude but then he feels sorry afterwards. With four men in the room, plus Bob, I just walk out. I feel like I am invading a man's world.

There is so much to see here but it would not be in our heart to go touring. Our feet are bad from doing so much walking. We walk up and down steps for Dave's room is on the third floor. The elevators are out dated and take too long. So we are walking and walking—with bad feet … in pain. We are able to get things at the PX now, which is a break for our personal needs. We are still planning on going home but we don't like leaving Dave. We hope he will make friends here so he won't be lonely. We hope and pray that he will do well after we go home. We love him so much and it will be hard to leave him. It was hard when he left Philadelphia to go to Germany the first time. Bob thinks I ask too many questions about what is going to happen with Dave when we leave. Bob does not understand how I feel about just leaving here without any information on Dave's recuperation. Praise the Lord for He has taken care of us since we have been here. He has put good people into our life to help us. We need prayers to get us all home safely now. Praise the Lord for He is good.

Oct 12, 1986

We got up early so we could go to Mass at the hospital chapel. Fr. Walsh had invited us to go out to lunch with him after Mass. During the "exchange of peace" Fr said that this would be our "goodbye Mass" for he knew that we were leaving the following Wednesday. He was a wonderful support to us since we first met. We all had been touched by his gift of the Holy Spirit. Dave liked him too. He told us that he would be picking us up at our hotel at 11:30. It was a cooler day today. Just like fall should be. The church bells were ringing off and on all morning, calling the faithful ones to Mass. Fr. was right on time to pick us up. He took us to the next town to see how other people lived. This was along the Rhine River, which is very famous. This was a very old town and was quite different from what we had been seeing for the last three weeks. Fr. said he would show us a church that is 1000 years old. He took us to an old German Restaurant that had very good food. He told us that he liked being in the military as he did not have any family left but an aunt in New York, where he originally came from. He had some funny stories to tell. Bob liked him a lot. He was just one of the neat people that God put into our life at this time of stress. God knew that we needed someone who understood what we were going through. He even got Bob to receive the Holy Eucharist while we were attending mass there. Fr. knew his job really well. He was filled with the Holy Spirit. It was an afternoon well spent. Thanks be to God for putting so many nice people in our life when we needed them. Fr. took us back to our hotel to rest before seeing Dave. When we got to the hospital he did not miss us as he had a nice nurse tech taking care of him. She had washed his hair and cleaned his face of more glass. She was doing a good job with him. He looked much better. He liked all the attention he was getting. Each day he was getting stronger. Praise to God for all our prayers were getting answered.

Oct. 13, 1986

I started my day with the Rosary, as usual. I had a good nights' sleep last night. It's a nice sunny day today but on the cool side. I went to breakfast by myself, as Bob likes to sleep in. After breakfast I went downstairs to do wash so I would not have a lot of dirty clothing to take home. Bob told me that Dave was teasing him that "because he was so busy when he was little" that now he has to push him around in the wheel chair. Now he was his buddy and has his whole attention. Bob had him laughing so much on Sunday that his broken ribs were hurting. It was good to have some fun. He seemed more like the old Dave we knew and loved.

Oct. 14, 1986

We started the day by going for a walk down the hill for our last look at Wiesbaden shopping area. We did some shopping and had some food that we knew we would not have at home. Pretzels and cheese bread were sold on the street. We had coffee and cocoa in one of the little shops. I got a new blue sweater. We looked for things for our trip home. We had a good time.

The cobble stone streets are hard to walk on and hard on our feet. It was a beautiful sunny day. We finally got back to the hospital to see Dave. He was looking really good now. We stayed with him until 8 pm. It will be so hard to leave him. This would be our "goodbye visit.". We tried to get Dave ready for our leaving here but it still was hard leaving him not knowing what was coming next for him. We knew that it was going to be a long recovery. Knowing the care he has received up to this point; we were hoping for his full return to good health.

Oct. 15, 1986

We were picked up by Sergeant Donovan and Wanita who we met before. We had trouble at the gate at the airport due to the fact that there were many people waiting for passes. We were concerned about making the plane but the sergeant called ahead and we were greeted by a hostess who checked our bags and took us to a VIP room until everyone got onboard. We were then taken to the plane. We didn't have to wait in line. We were told not to worry. For some reason the plane did not take off right away. Sergeant Donovan could not leave until 30 minutes after our take off for it was her job to see that we were in the air. She told us this so that if anything changed she would be there to take care of us. Our plane was a North Western plane 747. It was very comfortable.

We did have a good trip home. It went faster than I thought it would. I was glad that we were going to Philadelphia instead of New York, closer to home. Robert Jr. and his friend, Rickey, picked us up at the airport. Pam, our daughter-in-law, had dinner waiting for us. The grandchildren were glad to see us home too. We had all kinds of welcome home signs waiting for us. It was good to be on our own home grounds again. We were mixed up for awhile and Bob had to go back to work the next day. I was still upset with rashes and infections all over my body. I would have to make an appointment right away. Dr. Bub had me on medication before we left to help me through it. My nerves were getting the best of me with all this stress. Rose was very understanding. She always has been there for me and knows my feelings. It is good to have friends to depend on who know you so well. Terri has been a big help too. We are blessed with so many good friends. We call Dave often and I write him every day even if it's just a little news. Everyone is very concerned about Dave's condition and are still praying for him. His troubles were far from being over but at this time we did everything we could. Now it was up to him and our good Lord's healing power.

OUR MASTER PLAN
BIRTHDAY 1986

Happy birthday to you! Birthdays, birthdays … what is all the fussing about? Each year everyone has one. It is a day to remember the day you were born. Most important, it is the day that the Lord decided for you to come into the world. Some people are reminded about it and some want to forget it. Some people cannot face the fact that they are getting older. Some birthdays are happy but some can be sad. The best thing to remember is to be glad you are given another time to celebrate again. However; some birthdays are marked special because of making that "special age". Some people would rather not note it at all. What we all need to do is count our blessings that you have more time to get done what God wants you to do on this earth. Only God knows the end to our birthday times, for the day will come when he calls us home to him. Meanwhile, enjoy each birthday you have here on earth by spending good times with people you love. Time is our most precious gift from God. So use it wisely.

This year was different for me from last year. All the children took me out to dinner and we shared a meal together. Giving of their time to be with me on my birthday was nice. Most of the time Bob has the family over at our house, so this was less work for us.

One of the hardest birthdays I had was when we had to rush to Germany to be with David. He was in a bad car accident. We were getting ready to celebrate my birthday with a big party. But instead I spent it in a foreign country away from my family. It just goes to show you that birthdays can be hard when you are not around the ones you love.

OUR CHRISTMAS JOYS OF 1986

We always played Christmas songs while putting up our Christmas tree and decorating the house. I always use my Christmas cards that I get in the mail; for each one is special. Many Christmas Eve's were spent wrapping gifts since I had so much else to take care of during the day. All our family comes together on Christmas Day to share a good meal and exchange gifts. This year in 1986, Kate Lynn was almost a year old and Trish Ann was three. She didn't know much of what was going on. We got a message that Aunt Rose's Mom had passed away after a long battle with cancer.

David was home on leave from the Air Force. I had made his favorite dinner. He hadn't been home for a holiday for a long time. I had asked Rose and her family over since it was a sad time for them. Diane had come to help make cookies two days before Christmas. Of course, she wanted to learn how to make them. The holidays went along quite well.

We had just about got the holidays behind us when we got invited to Uncle Rudy's country club for a surprise 60th birthday party for his wife, Aunt Dotty. It was a very nice party of about 56 people. He had a great dinner, surf and turf, and a band too. Dotty was really surprised and happy after she got over the initial shock. The dancing was fun too. I didn't know many people there but Bob did since he used to work in his brother's real estate office. The evening was a very special one; one that we will remember for a long time.

One of the saddest times of the season was when we had to go to the funeral for Aunt Rose's mother, which was right after Christmas. They had a service at the funeral home but nothing in church. We did said prayers for her and her family. Our priest, Fr. Harry, came to support Rose and her family. It was good of him to be there. A luncheon followed the service. What a way to end the season. But, life must go on!

David was home from the service but he was out with his friends most of the time, like young people do. He would soon be returning to Germany but will be out of the service in the spring. He has been through so much since his car accident. We were just glad that he is doing so well. He still has a cast on his leg but at least it's in the healing process.

Well, it's time for some good news. We have settlement on the land that we purchased from Bob's brother. We have decided to build our own house. We will be leaving the home that we have lived in for the past twenty years. After many prayers, we decided that Upper Macungie was the place to go. This was really starting out new. It will mean a new church and new friends. It will be hard to leave St. Paul's church. Our children have all grown up here. We have a lot to remember about how God has worked in all our lives and all the support we have received from good Christian people. I myself will be giving up a lot for I am very much a part of St Paul's loving Christian community. I have a lot of friends that I will miss. I feel the Lord has a plan for us and He will help us to adjust. Our new life will be with St Joseph the Worker in Orefield, Pa. Time will tell when this all will take place. I know I will miss being a part of an active prayer group, but I will visit whenever I can. They are my Christian family and always will be. If you search with your heart, you will find the right people to be with. I also feel that change brings growth and I feel that this is part of God's Master Plan for us. In life we have joys and sad times but with it all comes more adventures for us.

On the last day of the year we ended up at Bob's brother, Rudy's house for a New Year's celebration and also Bob's birthday. His brother had invited his whole family so the house was filled with family and friends. Rudy liked to play old records and dance to the tunes of the 40's. To us this was boring. Everyone was dancing and singing and there was lots of food and drinks. We ended up watching a family movie from a long time ago. This was an old eight millimeter film from long ago but it was funny to see them dancing and having a good time just like we were. Most important we were all together just being ourselves. Bob got a surprise, his brother had a cake for his birthday, and we all shared the joy of another year together. It was a nice way to end the year with laughter and singing and looking forward to the New Year.

God is so good to let us be a part of a happy family. By the time the party ended it was 3 am. On New Year's Day Robert Jr. came over with his family to share dinner. I told them not to forget that we would be having supper for David on Sunday as he was leaving for Germany on Monday. We all wanted to be there to say goodbye again and tell him we would be praying for his safe return to his base in Germany.

A little note regarding the end of 1986, I want to thank God for letting us have good friends and family who have supported us through our ups and downs. It is a wonderful gift to have friendship of a lasting kind. We did a lot of traveling even after Bob's foot surgery. Thanks to our good friends we got to the seashore many times. We enjoyed them all. We both turned fifty this year and the Lord has more for us to do on our journey together. Let's hope the year 1987 is filled with more good blessings. Only our Master knows what is the best path to take. With our minds and hearts open to His will, we will be looking for that rainbow (God's gift) to let us know it is going to be OK.

OH HAPPY DAYS LONG AGO

Christmas is my favorite holiday. Even when I lived with my Dad, he would tease me and say he was not going to put up a tree at all. Then on Christmas Eve, after I was asleep, he would do it all by himself. In the morning there it would be with lights and tinsel.

Snow was on the streets when we walked to Midnight Mass. I was cold but we bundled up with knitted hats, gloves, boots, and ski pants. This was a special service. The choir was singing so beautifully. It truly was a Holy Night. We were very tired when we got home. I would be so excited about what I would find under the tree in the morning. We were lucky if we found new socks and underwear. We also got ribbon candy and candy canes. Children today have so many toys that they do not know which one to play with. I know why Christmas is very important to me. I get to share it with my children and grandchildren. I love doing things for them. It brings me joy to be able to cook dinner and buy gifts for everyone. I love to decorate with the Nativity and Santa. I will always have a tree. Every year it is different, even with my old favorites. I have lots of decorations that people have given me over the years. I put them up and remember all the love that went into that gift. This adds to the joy of the holidays. Bob and I are happy to have had all these years to share with our family and friends. God has been so good to us. It will be forty-five years of celebrating the Lord's birthday with all his blessings. He has the season filled with joy and love.

INTRODUCTION

MY TRIP TO LOURDES, FRANCE 1987

Your life in the past can help you do greater things in this life in the present. God has a great plan for us in our lives if we let Him lead us. Trusting in Him will get you through it all. We are truly in His hands.

I recall saying after my children left the nest, "So what will I do now". My time as a mother was at rest as this was how the Lord worked this new path into my life. This was my reward for sharing His mother with others, another gift to share with me on my journey. Yahweh called me to a wonderful part of my journey showing me a bit of heaven here on earth. How great You are to make this trip possible for me. You gave me a choice but you knew that I wanted to go. I often thought that I would like to go to Fatima but I did not think I would get the opportunity to ever go to Lourdes, France to visit Our Lady of Lourdes Shrine.

My grandmother once told me the story of St. Bernadette when I was a little girl and I always planned on going there to see for myself this beautiful place she described. How nice of God to let me overhear that this trip was being offered. Because this was the Marian year, we were trying to spread the devotions of Mary everywhere. We were sharing the traveling Mary statue visiting different families in the parish with those who wanted to have it displayed. The rosary was prayed each day for a week. Many talks were given on the Rosary to encourage them to pray everyday. Now I was going to see for myself, this great place of devotion. Thank you Lord for granting me the opportunity to be your vessel for the work you wanted accomplished during this mission.

TRIP TO FRANCE

It was in the spring time that I first heard about an offer to go on a pilgrimage to Lourdes, France to visit Our Lady of Lourdes Shrine. I was talking to someone after Mass and was told that Father Harry was looking for someone to be a companion to a lady who wanted to go to Lourdes, France. The trip would be free of cost. I spoke to Father Harry about it. I told him I would have to speak to my husband, Bob, to see how he felt about my going away for nine days. After talking to my husband who agreed it would be good for me to go, I called Father Harry back to say that I would like to meet with the woman I would be going with. Father Harry gave me the number to call to get the details of the pilgrimage. I could hardly believe this was going to happen. I was amazed Bob, my husband, agreed I should go.

My next step was to meet the person that I was going with. The more I talked about the trip, the more I felt that I was meant to go. Little did I know that the person who was to be my companion was in a wheel chair and needed a lot of special care. I made an appointment to meet with Loreen and her mother.

On my first visit with them, I was welcomed in their home and we seemed to hit it off right away. One of the reasons Loreen's mom could not go was because she had a bad back and it would be hard on her. She knew she could not do all that needed to be done for Loreen on that long trip. Loreen had gone to France before and she wanted to return again. She was very faithful to Our Blessed Virgin Mary and she shared why she wanted to go to this holy place.

Loreen had a disease that caused nerve damage to her spine so she is in a wheelchair. This also caused a breathing problem for her so she had a tube in her throat. She did need help with all these things. I had given up my nurse's aid work but it would now come in handy for these tasks that needed to be done for Loreen.

While waiting for Loreen to join us for lunch, her mother shared with me that her daughter was a very fussy person about how things should be done regarding her care because she was a nurse before her illness set in. I agreed that I would work with her all summer so I could get to know all about her needs. I also wanted to know her better and know what I was to do while she was in my care.

Loreen had just finished her bath with her nurse's aide and then she came into the living room to meet me. I was invited to eat lunch with them so we could get to know one another. We also went over the plans for the trip. I had never worked with a person who had this type of handicap but I was willing to learn how to clean the tubing that was in her throat. This was a very tedious task and had to be performed properly in order to prevent infections.

Loreen had a good sense of humor for someone who had all these problems to deal with. I made visits all summer with Loreen and her mother. I kept praying that we would be able to get along together for this trip. She owned an electric wheel chair which helped her to be as independent as possible in order to get around. She thought it would be the best way to go. We talked about our trip in great detail which included a limo service to take us to the airport in New York where we would be getting on a chartered flight to go to France. This plane was filled with nurses, doctors, priests, and brothers who were all volunteers to deal with the sick that came from all over the country.

On the morning of our departure, we were filled with joy and excitement in anticipation of what was to come. The limo arrived on time to pick us up and transport all our luggage and belongings, including a wheel chair, which had a very heavy battery. Loreen was determined to take this wheel chair with her. The limo driver was very understanding and concerned about our welfare. Now her mother would get a rest from all the responsibilities for the nine days we would be away.

On our arrival at Kennedy Airport, I remember the first problem we ran into was at the ladies room. The handicap facilities were out of order so this meant I had to ask others to assist me in getting Loreen into the regular bathroom which was not an easy task. The Lord was good to me for we met up with a very kind woman who helped us. We found out later that she was on our flight. This was just the beginning of many other things to happen. The Holy Spirit was working His power of prayers.

The next problem was that the battery for her wheelchair needed to have a special check-in with lots of paper work to get it on the plane, due to the fact that it contained acid. Finally we were able to board the plane. All the sick were placed on the plane first, so Loreen and I had to be separated for awhile. The priests that were with us were from the Dominican order and dressed in white robes. There were also Brothers with us also, who were very helpful to everyone. Seeing we were a chartered flight, we were on our own time. We all had to have badges on so they knew who we were and we could be identified. We also had passports.

Loreen had her first humbling experience as one of the Brothers carried her in his arms to her seat. He put her in a place where she could use three seats so she was able to lay down to sleep because this was an eight hour flight. I was in the same row so I could be near her.

After we were all settled in, Father Paul, one of the Dominican Priests, began our trip by praying the rosary. I learned that there were a lot of volunteers who were on board to help the sick and anyone else who needed help. We had a good trip, for everyone was friendly and kind. Some families traveled with their loved ones. Each person had their reasons for wanting to go on this excursion. Some of them do this every year. I did some reading this summer about where we were going in France.

I knew of the story of St. Bernadette since I was a child but I never dreamed that I would get to go to this beautiful place. I was very happy that I was going to this historical place. Everything was different on this airplane ride. It was special to see the faith of the people who were going there for healing at Our Lady of Lourdes Grotto. I remember the sunlight coming through the plane window as we were getting ready to land in France. This time the sick had to wait for us to get off the plane first because they had to be transported off the plane in a certain way. I was worried about leaving Loreen again but Father Paul told me that we were both going to the same hotel. Loreen insisted she was going to a regular hotel while the other handicapped people were going to a place called hospice which was a hotel for the sick. She registered at the regular hotel thinking that we could cope with her conditions there, which of course was a mistake. She felt that I would be able to care for her at the regular hotel as if she was cared for at her home, which we found out was not the case the very first night of our stay; however we were not aware of what was waiting for us.

It was wonderful to watch these people work with the sick. They knew just how to handle each and every case. They were specially trained to do this work. Loreen and I were parted again. Father Paul reassured us that we were going to the same hotel. I had to go on a different bus because I had to claim the battery for her wheelchair. This was all extra paper work, but the staff helped with this issue.

Another problem we were not aware of was that electricity is very costly in France so the battery for the wheelchair became another issue to solve.

The next problem we encountered was that the humidifier in the hotel needed for moisture at night for Loreen's breathing, needed an extra long extension cord which the hotel did not have. They told us that the humidifier required electricity from the hall which was going to be a very costly item to run every night. We didn't know how we were going to get an extension cord; the humidifier had to be near her bed. I had all these concerns to deal with and I did not know what to do. By the end of this day, I felt like I had worked for hours. I was very stressed getting settled in. We had all our meals taken care of in the hotel as the meals were all included with the trip. We only had one night at the hotel together because we were told that Loreen should be at the hospice for all the care she needed so we discussed it and came to the conclusion, and knew what we had to do.

The next day, one of the Brothers helped us get Loreen to enter into the hospice plan. There were nurses and doctors there to help with what we did not have at the hotel. All these things were not in our plans but it was better for Loreen had all her needs taken care of by hospice. It was not far from the Grotto where all the activities took place. Everything was planned for Mass and prayer times. After eating my breakfast, I would go and get Loreen for the activities of the day. We were together until she would get tired or it was meal time.

On the first day, we rested for a while and then we took our first trip down to the Grotto. We were so happy to go where the Virgin Mary had appeared to St. Bernadette so many years ago. The rosary was being said there in the afternoon which gave everyone time to settle in. We found the Grotto just like they told us it would be, it was very beautiful. There were a lot of people everywhere. We didn't want to miss anything. There were many Masses said at different times of the day but you had a time set for your group to attend them.

At night, the procession had six thousand people all holding lit candles and singing "Ave Maria" together. It was a wonderful thing to be a part of this Holy experience. People came from all different countries from all over the world. Every day, people came with bouquets of flowers to place at the feet of Mary. It was their way of saying "I love you Mary".

One of the activities is to go into the water that comes from the blessed spring water. They had special tubs which you go into naked, but you were first sent to a private area to get undressed where women helped you get into a blue robe. The reason for this custom was to be like Christ, to be stripped and then walk through the cold water as a sacrifice. You prayed the whole time which was only about two minutes. Then the blue robe was put back on you and you were taken back into the dressing area.

This water comes from the spring water that Mary showed St. Bernadette when in a miracle, she appeared to her. Many people come daily to get their water for cooking and drinking. It keeps them going and healthy. This has been their water supply all these years. The miracle of the shrine has not stopped, nor has it ever run dry.

I asked Loreen if she wanted to be put into the water and she said not yet. She wanted to wait a few days and see how it was done. We were told that the water is very cold. Volunteers of men and women help you walk through the water and they also pray with you throughout the service by praying with you. Loreen knew she would have to take her brace off her leg and she was nervous about that. Everyday we would watch others go into the special rooms where it all took place. Many people assisted others with this event every day. Finally we agreed to participate. We went to the special room and were given blue robes to cover our naked bodies while we were going into the water. This was in honor of Mary's color, blue. The ladies who helped were also in blue. There were steps leading down into the water.

The sacrifice after the robe was removed was that you walked across the water praying that you could do it. You were to offer up whatever you were praying for at that time. By the time you completed the walk, you were back into the robe and warm again. Then you got dressed. While putting your clothing on, you get this very warm anointing from the Lord, blessing you for having the faith to go there in the first place. It was a great experience.

For Loreen, it was a little different; she had to be put on a lift and then gently placed into the water. She was covered with a blanket until she was put into the water for she could not walk. She wanted to be healed. She felt the warmth come over her too. It was good for both of us. I prayed for her also. Sometimes you get a different kind of healing, which is good for our souls and it sometimes happens after you get home or even years later in God's time, not ours. This is why we came for the unusual happenings.

One day, I was going to meet Loreen for the Way of the Cross prayer time. As I entered the elevator by myself, I was greeted by a brown mouse. I screamed and it ran away. When I told Father Paul about the incident, he laughed and said "he was just catching a ride down to the kitchen for something to eat, he won't hurt you, he is a French mouse".

On some days Loreen was happy but she did not like it because we were not together but it had to be that way because of all the care that she needed. One afternoon she wanted to go shopping for things to bring home. We went to different stores. We did get a few nice things and it was a nice time. Loreen became tired out and wanted to go back to hospice to get some rest.

After dropping her off, I did a little shopping on my own. On the street selling homemade cookies was a Carmelite sister. I did not think she would talk to me but she did. She said that the cookies were made by the sisters so they could give the money to the poor people. She was the only one who came out to the public. She asked me if I had ever been to Europe before and I said yes, last year, and it was because of my son Dave's car accident in Germany and that he was still not healed. So she kindly said that she and her sister would pray for him. This is a good example to show how God is so good for she did not have to take an interest in my story but she knew I needed to hear that he would be on the prayer list. When I got back to the hotel, I shared with Father John who I met and he said she is called the cookie sister and he knew all about her. He also said that it was alright to give her money but that I should watch out for the gypsies because they will rob you and that I should be careful with my purse for even by the Grotto, there is evil around. On the next day, while walking around, who do I meet, but a gypsy woman holding a baby and saying "baby hungry". She was begging in the street. I walked away because Father John told me to be careful. Not everyone is holy in this holy place. We were nine days in France, and for some reason, it was a very hot fall time. It was usually cooler this time of the year. One day, the temperature hit 106 degrees.

The day before we were to go home, Loreen was in a bad mood and she became angry with me but I did not know why. She was having a bad day. I asked her if I should come for her for the night prayers and she said no, that she wanted to stay there and watch from the porch. So I went back to the hotel and I was very tired and hot. I said to Loreen that I would see her in the morning and she agreed. I knew that she was unhappy, maybe she was a little homesick, but she asked me to leave as she was going to rest. I felt badly about leaving her in that mood but it was her choice.

I went to the procession by myself. I thought that I could find our group and it was not hard to find them in the dark because of the red, white, and blue candles showing me the way to go. I found all the people from our group and they asked about Loreen. I told them she was too tired to come tonight. After the prayer time, I was very tired, so I walked back to the hotel after praying for my son Robert who was in the hospital since Tuesday when I found out he was there. I could not go to him until we got home the next day. I did want to say some extra prayers by Mary to ask her to help find out what was wrong with him. By the time I started to walk back to the hotel, I was very tired and hot. All I remember was that I got to the elevator doors, and then I passed out. I had fainted for the first time in my life. Somehow, someone found me and called the group leader and when I came to I could hear a woman talking about packing my things. It was no one that I knew at that time. I looked up and there was Father

Paul standing there at my side. He asked how I was. I asked him what happened. He said that they found me passed out in the elevator. I looked at my hand and saw a medal of St. Theresa in my palm which happened to be my favorite saint. Such a powerful experience proves how God is always watching over us. I hugged Father Paul and whispered I was sorry to put them through all this. He said, my child, you have to go to hospice now so we can make sure you are alright. The nurse will bring you over in a wheelchair. You are not to walk now. Then it came to me, I said, Oh Father, what did I do with Loreen, and he said she is at hospice. She is just fine and you did not leave her any place but there. Because we had that disagreement, I thought I left her somewhere. I was mixed up but the nurse said you have been under a lot of stress and this is why you passed out We all go home tomorrow so you will be just fine. The nurse took me and the suitcase in the wheelchair for she said I was still too weak to walk. Once we got to hospice, I went to bed and to sleep very quickly. I had additional stress when I called home and found out that my oldest son was in the hospital and that they did not know what was wrong. So I had a lot to pray for again. Everyone was so good to me. I was in good hands. The staff took care of everything at the hotel. I would be leaving from hospice in the morning

The staff got up at 4:00 am to prepare the patients in readiness to go home. The sick had to be ready to go by 6:30 am in order to get them to the airport, after a hard job the day before of packing all their supplies and belongings. Now the patients had to get ready for the trip. This truly was great work on the part of the staff. Father Paul started with the Rosary then he said Mass. We then started out to the airport by buses in the dark because the sun was not up yet. At last there was coolness in the air which we had not had for our eight day stay here. One day, the temperature hit 106 degrees but the Lord sent cool breezes at night. Our group knew each other better now than when the trip first started. Each one was giving of themselves in different ways. It is truly God's army working in His kingdom. Many priests and nuns were onboard. It was amazing how they moved the sick people. At first it seemed strange, but now I realized it is best for the patients to be moved this way. They got the best care with caring people. I felt that I did not have enough information on what was going to happen. On the plane it was constant care and much concern for the sick.

In the morning, I saw Loreen and we made up about the day before. She wondered why I was there at hospice because we were to see each other at the airport but I told her we would discuss it on the plane. We both said we were sorry about the angry words spoken the day before. The rest of the trip was fine. The staff had a lot of work to do for the patients as they had to be prepared for transporting them back to the airport. Many prayers were said on the way home. Many people wanted to stop in Ireland during the fueling stop because the shopping was great there, but there would only be a fifteen minute stop so everyone rushed their shopping in ten minutes. Some felt it was not worth the stress of rushing their shopping to get things from Ireland so some did not get off the plane during the fuel stop. I decided to stay with Loreen because we had already done our shopping at the shrine.

The volunteers on the plane work under a lot of stress. Each person does loving things for each other. Some exchange medals, candy bars, etc. So much love is present. How beautiful your kingdom is Lord while on a pilgrimage. Everyone shares with each other. Some keep coming back every year. My dear St. Bernadette, you started something very good and you did not know it. Many people are aboard and they see the Lord's work being done. Even the young are very much a part of this plan. A man from England on the plane stated that he had never been on this type of plane trip before. He felt honored to be with us. All the nurses were well trained, loving, and concerned. The people were open and free-flowing with their love for each other. My partner on the plane was truly sent from God. She shared with me that she goes to Lourdes every year. She brings back the holy water to share with others. She witnessed her own healing. She was from Medford, Massachusetts near Boston close to where I was born and grew up.

A story was told that St. Bernadette while in the convent sewed cloth hearts and sent them out to people who did not have a heart and needed a new one. Another friend shared they had a son that disappeared and was lost and never came back home. The parents could not find any peace within themselves until they heard about a grotto in Portland, Oregon where Catholics gathered in honor of God's mother Mary with roses. This was the only place where they could at last find peace and quiet even though they were not of the Catholic faith. They found the retreat at the grotto was a place of beauty on a mountain side where spring waters were flowing quietly. I shared the word grotto which means roses with this man and he shared a place of peace that had a grotto and roses in the USA.

Our return trip to New York was smooth and enjoyable. It was a good flight. Praise the Lord. We could hardly wait to get picked up by our limo service which was a big disappointment for a man with a van appeared instead of a limo. Loreen was not happy about the van. She had ordered the limo and they sent a van instead.

I was very tired but burning with desire to share my experiences of this trip with everyone. The chauffer who picked us up at the airport was of the Baptist faith and asked us what country did we return from. I went on to share the trip to France and the grotto. He explained the word grotto means Rose to him. I told him that many people bring bouquets of roses to Mary to honor her.

However, it was a safe trip home. Loreen's mom was glad to see us. I took a lot of photos and assured her I would bring copies to them next week. After Loreen was settled in, I called my husband Bob to come and pick me up. While waiting for him, we talked about all the things that happened on our journey. One of things we found interesting was their custom of carrying the sick in blue buggies to the grotto and the spring waters. We had lots to share because so much had happened while we were away from Allentown for nine days. It was a trip like no other I had ever been on.

Our trip had many joys and lots of time to pray. I could say it was a giant retreat but it had many moments of trials just as every day life has its ups and downs, so did this trip. One of my fond memories of the grotto was to see the sunrise come over the mountains which reminded me of the Lehigh Valley mountains where we live. It is a beautiful place. I did not need an alarm clock there because I would wake up to the clicking sounds of ladies shoes on the cobblestones going past the hotel. It was their morning routine to get their holy water from the springs. The local people use this water for cooking their food and drinking for good health. I also knew it was time for the first Mass and prayer time before our day would begin.

The whole experience in France was so different from home. I did get a little home sick but I knew I had to be here to care for Loreen. When I heard about my son in the hospital, it made it harder for me to stay here as I was anxious to get home. I really trusted in God's blessings that everything would turn out alright. In the quiet of the morning I would go by Mary's shrine and pray. I knew that the nurses were taking care of Loreen and she was in good hands.

One of the things I found humorous about the rooms in the hotel near the grotto, was that the rooms are very much in demand. I had to hold a secret from the hotel that Loreen had gone to hospice because then a stranger would be put in my room and I did not want that. This is their policy to see that every bed is to be used at all times but no one said anything and I got through it.

All the Masses were said in several places and in different languages. Our main chapel was called Our Lady of the Rosary. The art work in the ceilings of this chapel was donated with money from the Bishops, Priests, and people of America. We were told where to go each day. We joined our group each night for procession to the Grotto, singing and praying while walking there. You knew where your group was located by the flags, banners and the lights with the names of the country on them. The good old glory flag was there for us. We knew where the Americans were. I could find them easy even with six thousand people in procession, for the USA sign showed me the way to them. I was proud to be an American and our red, white, and blue were there too. It made us think more about home to see the colors flying in the air. These are just a few of the things we shared with Loreen's mother. I would like to return again someday but do more touring of France as well as visit the grotto again.

As we finished talking about our wonderful trip, my husband arrived to pick me up with much anxiety due to the fact that I was away so long. Our Lord has a way of saying, yes my child, you have done my will. For me, a new cross to bear, for I was greeted with the news of my son still in the hospital being tested. We had to go see him immediately before going home first. Somehow I knew our prayers would be answered in God's time and not mine. Many years of miracles have happened since my son's illness. He is a walking miracle after being paralyzed before his surgery. A good man filled with his faith, which he has been a witness everyday, since I went to Lourdes. I know it was my miracle with extra blessings for going there.

TRIP TO ST. CROIX IN THE VIRGIN ISLANDS—1986

Our trip to St. Croix was different than our other trips to far away places. We went with friends, Mac and his girlfriend Barbara, who works with Bob. We left at 6:30 am by limo with a chauffeur, which was a great way to go. We arrived at Kennedy Airport two and a half hours before we had to board our plane. It gave us lots of time to relax and have breakfast in the lounge area. We got our boarding passes which enabled us to check in at American Air Lines. It was a big plane with ten seats across. Each trip we take gets bigger and better. We had all the comforts of home. We were offered a movie called "Rocky IV". Our meals and drinks were great too. The telephones which were available on the plane took my fancy. You know me with telephones. I would have liked to try them. Credit cards can do magic tricks even thousands of miles away. The phone was portable and you could take it to your seat if you wanted to. The standard rate was $7.50 for the first three minutes. That ruled it out for me. We had a good take off and landing. Kennedy is one of the biggest airports in comparison to landing in St. Croix which was so small. It was so hot while we were waiting to go to the rental agency to pick up a car. We had too many suit cases to fit into a rental car but I will learn to pack lightly one of these days, experience is the best teacher. Our driver from the rental agency was not very friendly. The ride from the airport was not too impressive. I remember Barbara saying, "so far I am not impressed". I agreed with her. We were judging by the poorer section of the island. After completing the paper work for the rental car we were off in an economy car which sounded like it was not going to make it up the hill. But due to the fact that Mac was used to driving sports cars, he was not happy about this car. We also had to drive on the left side of the road. Besides strange roads, the map said Route 66 but it turned out to be Route 86 which was what the sign read.

We had to drive around and up and down many twists and turns before we arrived at our Villa. The car had no air conditioning and the gas tank was almost on empty. Not knowing this area, we did get gas across the street from the rental Place. It was a good decision we made getting the gas here because the next station was far away. We only saw one other one near the villa. As we drove toward the villa we could see that we were following the sea shore line. This was filled with beautiful flowers and coconut trees along the way. I felt like I was driving in the little engine that could train because of the many curves. The roads went up and down like a roller coaster.

We finally reached the Reef which was what our villa was called. We checked in at the gate where a very dark fellow greeted us and told us where our home would be. We could see the golf course at the bottom of the hill. The villas were set against a small mountain which to us seemed like a little hill back in Pennsylvania. It was pretty, but most of the grass was brown due to the lack of rain. We finally found Villa 12 among about 100 villas on the property. Flowers and trees were everywhere. We also gave a smile to see that it looked a little more like the pictures we saw of the place shown to us by our friend who rented it to us.

Upon unlocking the door, we were hit with a new adjustment of the windows that were not working. This villa was not what we expected. One bedroom was upstairs and one was downstairs. It had two large full bathrooms. The kitchen and dining room was large. The living room was neat too. All the rooms had big ceiling fans and air conditioning. The patio was overlooking the golfing area and the bay. Our garden patio was a separate room which was outside and had a table and chairs. There were palm trees and bugs but this was the tropics so they were part of it. This place could use a good cleaning but we were tired and we made the best of it. I know we were spoiled by our other trips where the hotels were so different. We were on our own to do things for ourselves. We felt lost.

After getting settled in, we decided to hunt up the pool site and cool off. Bob and Mac took the car to go find some refreshments for the house. We were hoping they did not get lost. Barbara and I headed for the pool. We had to climb about fifty steps up a hill to reach the pool. Here was a beautiful large pool and only we were there. We found it sunny and breezy. The water was just like getting into a bath tub which suited me just fine. While waiting for the men to come back, we talked about our other trips that we had been on before in comparison to these arrangements. We agreed the other trips were better. I think right there and then we decided that renting our own pad was not the best way to go.

When the men returned, we talked about where we would go for dinner. We thought it would be best to go to a nearby restaurant which was at the bottom of the hill. It was called Duggans. We had a good dinner and we were there in about two minutes. We were sitting at an open tropical restaurant. We were sitting in large wicker chairs with high backs. We were all in casual clothing so we were relaxed. The menu had many American selections. This restaurant was run by a young man in his forties. We were glad to get back to the villa after dinner. It was about 10:30 pm so we all went to bed. We did check out the beach in the dark of the night. The dock also had a bar which was in a great setting for this island.

The morning sun was beating down on the patio and was very hot so most of the time was spent in our living room with the fan on. We ventured out to find a place to have breakfast in town which meant jumping into the car for a ride to a town called Christiana. On this road that was like a roller coaster, we landed at a shopping mall. We found a Wendy's that first morning. It was a clean place with good food. Everywhere was strange to us so we had to follow a map in order to get around. It was so hot we could hardly wait to get back to take a cool swim at the beach. We made a very important purchase. It was a Styrofoam cooler for our refreshments.

The drinking age is sixteen and you can also drink and drive with a beer in your hand. Everybody drinks beers and cokes because of the heat. I am so glad that I brought my supply of gum and life saver candy. We stopped at a convenience store for some food snacking stuff because we ate our main meals out.

The beach was not so nice because we were on the part called The Reef. The water contained these bugs called no seeums which stung you when you swam. It was also very rocky so we did not go swimming there again. We felt good about the pool because it was off season and there were not a lot of people there. We finally realized it was the heat that kept them away. In the winter most people came to the pool because it was cooler then. We did get burned the first day because we were not use to the tropical sun. It was very different than what we were use to. That was our weekend activity.

On Monday, we started out downtown again this time we parked our car by the docks which was filled with many sail boats and fishing boats. After breakfast at the Armor Inn, we decided to sign up for a sailing trip to a place called Buck Island, a national park in the ocean. The first thing the sales lady said was to make sure you cover up to prevent you from getting sun burned. The ship we were going to sail on was called The Virgin. We then took a ferry to the hotel on the bay where we had dinner that night. While having dinner, we asked the waiter if it ever rained here. His reply was it had not rained in four years. I told him I would pray tonight for rain. We all laughed about this but Bob said she prays for everything and usually gets an answer.

Monday was a relaxing day. In the morning, Mac was reading a flyer which gave him information about a dinner which included a Kettle Drummers performance which we thought would be something different to do so we decided to go. As we were getting dressed, I looked out the window and it was raining. Bob said why now, an answer to your prayer when we are going out tonight. This rain which was only going to be a shower turned out to be a little bit every day.

On a cloudy Tuesday morning, we set out for our trip to Buck Island. While waiting for our ships crew to get together we were looking over the area. It was very exciting to see everyone getting ready for this cruise. Our captain's name was Jim and his crew consisted of three island men, one of them was very well built. There was also a well built American girl named Kim. She was our hostess for the day. Alex Hamilton was second in command. One other man was our underwater guide for the under water park. It was real fun. At first we had to get fitted with flippers and masks with a breathing tube. I thought that I would not like it but I loved it. With my big lungs I had no trouble doing the under water stuff. We slowly sailed away from the town while our guides told us what we would encounter on this cruise.

There is some history of movie stars who have homes here such as Maureen O'Hara and others. The water used for drinking on this island comes from the ocean which is put through a process that takes the salt out of the water to make it drinkable. Because this island has very little rain most of the year, this is their only source of drinking water. The underwater park is protected by the government so that it is not disturbed by anyone to preserve its beauty. It is blue and green in spots, and very clear at the bottom. We sailed for about an hour and a half heading for a white sandy beach where our snorkeling lessons took place. The captain dropped the anchor. This is where we got ready for the dive. Everyone went into the water with their equipment on. Many young people were on this trip and were having fun. One of them was taking movies of all the action. We all lined up in groups for the underwater swim. It was a wonderful time down there for the fish were swimming with us. The colors were like a fairy land. We had to hold on to ropes so we would not get lost. I loved it. After our swim we had to get back to the ship. We were now going to a place called Shell Island for a picnic lunch prepared by the crew. They cooked fish over an open fire. Everything was ready for us when we got to this part of the island. It was very well planned. I don't like ship rides but this sailing trip was very relaxing. We all enjoyed it a lot.

The drinks were good. They were called Bahama Mamas. I thought they were fruit drinks but they had rum in them. I learned fast that there was a lot of rum in them because I started to get a little under the weather. The men were feeling no pain either. Bob's face got red and his head was roasting in the sun. He did wear his hat even though he hated hats. Both Bob and Mac had sunburns on their heads by the time we got back to shore. We finally got to Shell Island and I thought that it was going to be a beach area with collectible shells on the sand but it was a place to dump garbage shells after the meat of the shell is removed but it was neat to see any way. We had a lot of fun with the New Yorkers and we were all making plans to have a party that night. By the time we got back to the villa, we were wiped out and just went to bed without any dinner. Both Mac and Bob were complaining about their sunburned heads and each was moaning with Bob downstairs and Mac upstairs. It was like a choir chanting with pain from the tropical sun. Barbara had sunburn all over her legs and she could hardly walk the next day so we took her to the hospital emergency room. When they told her the cost would be expensive, she decided to take care of it herself when she got home.

Everywhere we went that week, there were little showers following us, but they didn't start till we were inside. When we came out, the showers had stopped. One local man that we met told us that we don't get rain like this. Bob told him I had prayed for rain knowing how much they needed it. The Lord is so good to us even on vacation.

With all the unusual things that happened on this trip, it turned out well. It was a learning experience but we would make different plans next time.

OUR FIRST TRIP TO FLORIDA 1988

It is now March 13, 1988 and we are getting ready for our trip to Florida in the morning. I cannot seem to get excited over this trip. This may be our last big vacation for a long time because we are building a new house this year.

We had some good traveling days even though it was cool and raining in North Carolina. The trees are in bloom here already. We had a lot of country music tapes which we enjoy listening to while riding in the car. We took Route 15 on the back hills of Virginia which we saw many beautiful farms with large beautiful homes. We had a nice dinner at a restaurant near the hotel on our first stop. I will say my rosary before going to sleep. Bob is watching his sports and a movie. I discovered you can get very tired just riding in the car. We have another day of travel tomorrow, so I might as well get use to it. Praise the Lord for a safe trip so far.

Our next stop was in Daytona Beach which we stayed the next night. We wanted to move on the next day so we could visit Uncle Rudy on the third day. We arrived at Uncle Rudy's to see his beautiful home. So far, since we left home, it has been cold. Today the temperature is going to be in the seventies. It was a long ride from Pennsylvania but with the stopping each night, it was tolerable. The beauty of God's world is all around us if we look for it and take the time to enjoy it. We are staying with Bob's brother who is renting a house there while looking to purchase a home. The house they are renting is right on the golf course so we can see golfers go by at different times of the day. Bob's brother is a good golfer so this is what he wants to do in the near future. We will be going out for dinner at the country club for the St. Patrick's Day celebration. I hope I find something green to wear. I am a little Irish on my mother's side of the family. I tried to call my sister Pat only to find out that her phone had been disconnected. I was disappointed not to be able to reach her. My brother lives near here also but I could not find his phone number. I will keep trying to reach them before we go home. Time will tell.

It is March 18, 1988. Here it is four days into our vacation and we have done a lot. Yesterday we spent part of our time in the beauty of God's world of nature. Bob and I went to a place called BAR Tower Gardens. This was a wonderful and peaceful experience. I felt like I was walking in the Garden of Eden or should I say wondering if Adam and Eve's garden was like this. When I walk around a place such as this, I know God's presence is so strong His spirit comes to my mind. I could see how "Mr. BAR" must have felt that way also. The flowers and trees were everywhere. The birds were singing. We worked up an appetite so we had lunch at the cafe' on the grounds. The temperature has gotten up to seventy today. The sun was so nice to enjoy after all the rain we had coming down here. In the south the people do not say it is cold but they say it is chilly today. So I learned something new. Everywhere we went; people were wearing green for St. Patrick's Day. Bob asked me what day it was. With all the days of traveling, we forgot to look at what day it was. I think somehow I mixed up my days with this story too. I wrote this on the eighteenth but then I jumped back to what we did on the seventeenth. After coming back to Rudy's house, we both took a nap.

I had a terrible headache from all the flowers and orange blossoms for I am allergic to them. The tower itself has an interesting history. It was built to hold the bells which play every half hour to add to the beauty of this place. We listened to the sounds of songs which were making the place more peaceful all around us. The orange groves are all around us too. Bob loves to see them. We took photos of these beauties. Some of the different things at dinner that night were the ice art at the buffet table. The chief had a clover shape in the center. The food was prepared with an Irish theme. They had corned beef and cabbage, green beer, and green cookies and the like. The cake had a green clover on it. We had green pea soup and lamb stew. All the desserts were in green. Key Lime Pie was another specialty. Many of the people present were wearing green shirts and ties and some had on green pants. These people really get into it and I am sure not too many were Irish. This was another world we were living in. In this club, we could see how the wealthy live. It makes you wonder. It is not my choice of life style. I like my own life and the values that we hold. We ended up with a good card game at home.

We are planning on going to see Epcot with Dot and Rudy today. We had a good time and we stayed all day.

Our first day, we went to visit St. Ann's church which Rudy knew I would like to see. There was a prayer tower outside of the church which was really something to see. We all prayed together. Bob and I lit a candle then we went inside.

Rudy said he would go to church with us on Sunday. God is so good to let us find this nice place to come and praise Him.

Before we knew it, it was time to head home but we did have a nice time and we got to know Dot and Rudy much better. Thank you Lord for all the good times you have given to us together.

OUR TRIP TO OHIO—1988

We wanted the whole family on this trip because no one in our family was doing this type of work. We planned for a month and a half to get ready for this trip. We were all going to Cincinnati, Ohio to witness our nephew Bob take his first oath for missionary work with the Glen Mary Order of Missionary Priests, We started out at 5:30 in the morning. We ran into some difficulties getting ready for travel. After everyone arrived, we found out that the van was not as big as we thought. We had many suit cases. We were looking at ten to twelve hours of togetherness. We had a twelve passenger van and there were four sisters, three brothers, and three sisters-in-law. We started out with a prayer lead by our dear sister in law Elva because she wanted us to have a safe trip. Some were talking and some were sleeping and Bob did most of the driving. I was thinking of this as a retreat but it was not my time of peace and quiet. Something was in the way of really being in the presence of the Holy Spirit. I knew our Lord was with us but I could feel the tension in it all. Bob did drive and his brother Rudy wanted to take over to give Bob a rest but that did not last long because he is not a very good driver. We were all holding our breaths. We had to check the map a few times for fear of getting lost. We finally did get to the motel in Ohio. It did not look so nice on the outside but once we got inside, it was really nice. We called his nephew Bob right away to make sure he knew that we were in town. We did make plans to meet with him for dinner. We all got settled in for our two day stay. After dinner we were invited to go up the hill for a party to meet Bob's friends and teachers and also the spiritual leaders. We felt a very warm welcome there. I could feel the love flowing. Jesus was present in all of them.

The life there was very simple. Fresh popcorn was made and smelled so good but we were all filled from dinner. Everyone was pleasant and cordial. Everyone talked to us like we were old friends already. Bob, my nephew, was so happy to have his whole family for his celebration. We were waiting for Tony, his brother, to appear but he was unable to make it. How disappointed my sister-in-law Sophie was that he could not attend because she wanted the whole family there. Many of her family were there for this moment of joy for her son. We also missed Vera our sister-in-law for she had to work and could not be with us.

Everyone dressed up really nice for the morning Mass and the taking of the oath day. It was a beautiful day to have the Mass service outside. Father called it God's cathedral of nature. It was a beautiful moving service. The sun was warm, yet there was a gentle breeze blowing. The birds were singing with joy. The moments of silence during the service was very touching for this is when we felt the spirit of God with us. At the Mass, we were all at peace. I felt the presence of our Lord on this holy ground. Sophie really looked her best carrying the offertory to the altar. She had her son and daughter in law with her. Three other young men were taking their vows also. We met Father Ruff who was the president of the Glen Mary's missionary; he was so friendly to us. After the Mass was over, we were filled with joy for Bob was on his way to a new step in his work for the Lord.

At the luncheon, everyone shared with us. Bob showed us around his home where he had been living and studied for a whole year. It used to be an old farm house so it made a good place for these men to enjoy a humbling experience. The house sits on a hill with great trees all about the land. The room down stairs was their chapel which had a large window which let the sun shine in with beauty of colors. Bob also shared with us that when it snowed in the winter, it makes a beautiful picture. It displays the snow lying on the windows ledge appearing to look like something out of a book. His bedroom was very simple for the mission-aries take a vow of poverty, which they are taught from the beginning.

It was interesting how Satan interrupted the joy of this occasion. It took a lot of effort to keep us cool. Some people don't understand how Satan tries to get into the circle of joy when people are close to God. We were tested every step of the way.

The next day we headed home after having lots of fun together as a family. Bob came to say goodbye at the hotel. He was very happy at this time.

THE ANGEL SHOP PROJECT

The year was 1995 when I got a call from our Lord to help with the Angel Shop Project. It all started while I attended a meeting at my church, St Joseph's, in Orefield. A woman was coming to ask our help to raise funds for a place called Mary's Shelter. This was a home for unwed mothers and their babies. She needed a lot of help to get this started, plus lots of cash. She talked about the work that had already been done for the shelter. My mind was going a mile a minute by this time. I wanted to be a part of whatever we did. We talked about possibly opening a store for Religious items. I mentioned that Angels are very popular and could we possibly build on that idea. Other ideas were mentioned and Jan said she would think about it all and get back to us. She asked us to pray that we did what God wanted us to do. I had always wanted to open a business of some kind. Finally, after several days passed, Jan called and told us that she liked the Angel idea. Now we had to find a store that we could afford in a good location. We all started looking. In a few days we found one in a nearby shopping center.

Jan was paying for the first months rent to get us started. She also lined up one of her neighbors, Robin, to be the manager and bookkeeper. I would be the assistant manager. I was also wiling to look for volunteers to work the shop as well as to get donated items to sell. We were all so excited. I felt that this was my way of helping single moms and their babies get a good start in life. Jan wanted me to meet Robin, whom I would be working with, so we could get acquainted ahead of time. We had many details to work out. Finally, Jan got the call that we could go and see the shop, which it was painted and ready to go. We all went and agreed it was the right place. We had been praying for this to happen and now it was finally on go. Now we had to get to work.

We were filled with excitement that the Lord was helping us to make this happen. Many people had called us and wanted to be a part of this project. Jan suggested that we meet at her home to work out a schedule. This took place on August 17th. We also had asked craft people to come to our first meeting. God was sending many blessings our way. We kept on praying. As we entered the hall there was a table of items that were ready to sell. Refreshments were also being served. We started with a prayer and then got down to business. We had seventeen women there, which was a great start. Jan shared her story of Mary's Shelter and why we needed the financial support. Then Robin and I were introduced. We talked about our needs and our goals. A friend from church offered to order books and items for the shop. We all agreed to make it a customer friendly place. We wanted this place to be filled with Christian spirit. We even talked about serving free coffee and free wrapping. We would be looking for people to back us up for we knew that it would take a lot to get it off the ground. We hoped for help from the young people too. We would have three methods of getting items to sell which were: purchasing, consignment of crafts, and donations. Robin would enter everything into the computer. We had gotten some furniture given to us so we were off to a good start. Many miracles were happening with the store getting started the way it did. We really were on a shoe string budget. We prayed a lot so it would be successful.

We invited all the ladies to the dedication of Mary's Shelter which was taking place on September 8th. Bishop Welsh was doing the mass and then we would take a tour of Mary's Shelter in Reading, Pa. We were to be a part of the celebration and the joy of what was to come by our supporting efforts. The ladies were all open to new ideas about what we could do. We had to trust in the Lord and Our Faith would go on from there. The store was to open on October 2, 1995. We would also be selling greeting cards. I then added that I was bringing in a line of porcelain dolls so we would have something for little girls. I planned to have Angel dolls also.

One woman offered her husband to make gift boxes to be part of the free wrap. Another woman offered box spring and beds for the shelter. Another woman offered her husband to help set up the shop. Only with God's help could this be happening. Many details were coming together because people cared and were willing to get this done in Jesus' name. The more we prayed, the more we could see this happening. The Angel Shop was a dream come true for us. One woman offered her talents to make us a sign with a light in it for free.

When word got out through the church bulletins, we had many offers. One offer was for craft dolls from The Widdles Country Artisan. She was just a small business person but she wanted to help. Marie designed them herself. She had her shop in her basement. I made an appointment to go see the dolls the next week.

Her dolls were famous. She even had them in the Disney shop in Florida. She called us because we were a non-profit shop and she knew the money would go toward Mary's Shelter. It was wonderful to see all these dolls. She said I should pick out two of the dolls and she would give them to us free of charge. This was to be a small start but she ended up giving us many more. She became a good consignment person. She also had a line of Angel dolls. Perfect! This is how God helped me make a new friend while helping the shop also. Her dolls were a big seller.

Next I went to craft shows to see if I could get people to sell their items in our shop on consignment. Jan and Robin went to New York to the big craft show to get items for Christmas. We knew this would be our busiest time. Donations were great for this was pure profit. I remember the excitement Robin and I shared when we got the keys to the shop for the first time. We were happy to know that this was going to work. We thanked the Lord, for we could feel His presence and His blessings on us.

Jan came to see what else we needed to get the store open. She heard of a store in the mall going out of business. She went to the store looking for shelving and display cases. When they heard what she wanted them for they gave them to us free. They were worth $20,000. But we had to get them out by the end of the week. I got my son and his van and we all got our husbands to help. But we did it. Our team was working very hard to get ready for our opening in October. Our volunteer list was growing. This meant many hours on the phone making the arrangements. Things at home had to take a back seat for awhile. I knew things would calm down once we had everything set up and running.

Jan contacted some college students from St Francis College asking them to volunteer some of their time. They would be young people helping young people. So many actions were being done for us to make this a success in the name of Jesus and Mary. The Holy Spirit was touching many hearts and souls. Word was out.

A reporter, from a small newspaper, called me on the phone and wanted to know what we were about and all the details. We needed the advertisement! This was the first time I was ever interviewed by a reporter. The name Amelio was there in print. The reporter did a great job on the article. We needed to let people know why we were doing this. I explained that with the power of prayer, everything was getting done. We were all working together to help unwed mothers and their babies. All profits were going to them. This was our quiet way to help with the abortion issue. God's small reward for doing his will.

One night when I was working, a woman came in and asked a lot of questions about Mary's Shelter. She said she was a teacher and needed the information for one of her students who was pregnant and didn't know what to do. She was in her seventh month and hadn't told her parents yet. I gave her all the information. Later on I found out that this was the first baby born at Mary's Shelter. I was part of getting that woman a safe place to have her baby. Our shop was successful in many ways because we had faith filled people doing the will of God.

A couple of months passed and Jan wanted to have a thank you party for all who were helping. She made it special by asking the Bishop to come and bless the shop and our work. We even had TV coverage. It was a good time for all. One rule we made was never to open on a Sunday for this was a day of rest. We showed that we were a Christ centered store. I was part of the Angel Shop for five years. It was a chance to fulfill one of my dreams of having a store of my own, even if it wasn't. But I know I played a big part in working it like it was. I enjoyed it very much. We had our ups and downs but we kept going. Many friends were made over these years. This was very rewarding work. It is still there today. It will be 10 years old this year and we have moved from that area so I don't see it anymore but I know what good all this did for all who were a part of working with Angels of all kinds.

"I COULD BE MYSELF"
(LOVING CHILDREN)

In 1996 we lived in upper Macungie in a house that we had built in 1988. We loved it there. At this time I was running a business called "Grandma's Play Room". I started this business when my grandson, Cory, was born and my daughter asked me to watch him. I decided that if I was going to watch him everyday I might as well watch a few more. That's how it all started. I had just stopped working for Kmart, which was not the greatest place to be during the Christmas Holidays. Everyone gets on edge during this busy time of the year. The customers were demanding as well as the bosses who ran the store. I didn't want to spoil my happy time by putting up with them during the HOLY season. Our house was a ranch house with a large family room. I decided that this would be a great place to put a play room. It was all I needed to make it work. I put an ad in the newspaper, saying I would be taking children ages three and up. I also stated that I wanted children to come and enjoy playing in my Playroom. I believed that children can learn by playing with educational toys plus being in a safe place to be as well as having fun. In day care schools there is so much going on that they don't get to rest, only at story time and nap time. We did fun things but I let them pick and choose what they wanted to do.

My first call was from a mother who had two children for me to care for while she went to nursing school. She felt that my plan for the children was a good one. She had a little girl two and a boy four. I thought this would work out well, as I had Ryan, who was a little older than Cory but they were babies. So now I had four children to take care of. This was a full day for me even though they came at different hours. I always wanted to open a daycare. I did a lot of praying through the eight years that it was open. It was good to be able to help families from our church. Once the word got out, I had plenty of business, even after school children. These were very happy years for me. I had children in my life and I was helping families, knowing that their children were in a safe place. The parents were very good to me on holidays. But as all good things come to an end, I had to give this up. My body just wouldn't let me do it anymore.

"ANGELS WERE WITH US."

The car of our dreams is gone on a ride to the country. Yes, here it is December 11, 1996 and Bob and I are recovering from a car accident. On November 20, 1996 we went for a ride after lunch in the car with Christopher, our grandson, who was with us. It was nice to share this time together for Bob was always working overtime. So this was a chance to be away from the house for the afternoon. I said to Bob; let's go find the houses that they are always talking about on the radio. This was in Orefield, near our church, so I thought it would be fun to see this. It would be something to look at during a ride in the country. Bob said it was a nice day except for the clouds overhead. I thought it looked like a funny day too, but we headed out on the back road. We went down to Blue Barn Road to a stop sign. We did stop and the next thing I remember was seeing the glass cracking on the front windshield. I looked over at Bob and saw his head up high and his glasses hanging off his ear. We did not hear the sound of the crash but we were hit and we're being pushed off the road. Just that fast, my thoughts went to Christopher who was in the back seat. When we stopped, I pulled myself together and I asked Bob if he was hurt. I told him not to move until I could get some help. Bob was yelling that he could not move. He was pinned down by the seat belt crushing his groin, which he could not release. He was up against the door. I released my seat belt then pushed the door open. I went back to see why Chris was so quiet. A man stopped to see if he could help by calling the police. I told him my husband is hurt badly and cannot get his seat belt off. Someone came to help get Chris out of his seat. I was so nervous about Bob being hurt that I could not undo the belt. I was holding Christopher in my arms when an older woman came over to us and then I realized that she was the one who had hit us. I asked if she was hurt. She said she was having chest pains. She walked away saying we did not stop at the stop sign but I know we did.

Bob did stop at the stop sign but he did not see anything coming. When he proceeded to advance, he looked up thinking it was all clear. It all happened so fast. Her truck was so heavy and big that upon impact, it pushed us off the road and into a field. It was strange how we did not hear a sound on impact.

Our angels were all around us, for Chris could have been pushed out of the car but he was in his safety seat and that is what saved him. He had a good strong seat belt on, was belted twice, and was also seated in the back which helped save him from getting hurt. Our Pontiac was a strong car too. The safety belts saved us too.

When the police arrived at the scene of the accident, Christopher and I were in the back of the car and they asked us to sit in the rear of the cruiser to get the facts of the accident and find out who was hurt. Meanwhile, Christopher was jumping up and down saying Car go Boom, Car go Boom. He was only two at the time but he was not hurt at all. I had whiplash from the safety belt but it saved my life. While I was being questioned, the ambulance arrived and was preparing to take Bob to the hospital. They then prepared me with a neck collar and told me I had to go to the hospital in the ambulance to be checked. Christopher was placed in a car seat inside the ambulance to be with me. While transporting us all to the hospital, my daughter was immediately notified at the hospital where she worked so she made the arrangements for our care. Pam and Robby arrived with their children shortly after we were in the emergency room. Many x-rays were taken to evaluate our injuries. I kept asking about Bob because he was hurt more than I was. They just said he was being checked. The doctor came in and said he viewed the x-rays and said we could go home.

The miracles were just beginning because we had no broken bones just a lot of pain. Our days of pain were spent together. We were both on pain medications so we could get the rest we needed. Togetherness is what we had even though Bob was hurting more than I. The only place we went to was the doctor's office with someone else driving us.

Bob had to sleep in the Lazy Boy recliner for two weeks. He would keep trying to go to bed but it was too painful for him in the rib area. He was doing good but got some fluid in his leg which would cause him pain down his leg. Doctor Steward said he could have fractured his hip bone so she wanted him to be x-rayed again but nothing showed up. He just needed more rest.

Now we have all the paper work to deal with. Our new car deal went very smoothly. Our old car had been demolished. Due to the fact that we have a nephew in the car business, he helped us in our purchase of another vehicle; he saved us lots of red tape. Bob could not go car shopping due to the stress and pain of everything that happened during the accident. The insurance man came to see us and made out a check so we turned that over plus added more cash to get the newer car. It takes one step at a time to make things easier.

We had good people bring us meals and helped with whatever they could do for us. I had to put Grandma's play room on hold but the parents understood what we were going through so my kids would be back as soon as I could handle it. Thanks to God and the many prayers, we made it with us both back to good health.

OUR MASTER PLAN BIRTHDAYS

October 1999

My birthday was on October 4. On the Sunday before my birthday, my dearest friends, Rose and Geno, took us for a ride and then to dinner to celebrate my birthday. What a nice gift. We have not had much time together lately so it was fun to get together and catch up on what is new.

On the morning of my birthday, my day started out with the usual stuff until the phone started ringing with many calls from friends and family. We also had showers with thunder and lightning. Just to get my day started off with a boom! This is not the way I usually like to start my day, but God does have a sense of humor, so I had to deal with it. No nice walk to start my day. Since April, I have been walking everyday to get healthy. My legs are stronger now.

So many of my friends and family called, the phone was ringing all day. I got loads of cards. James called to say he would be bringing dinner. It was a lamb dinner from Wegman's. Bob got me a cake and a card. Even Doris called from Massachusetts. What does all this mean? I am blessed to have so many friends and family to remember me. All of my birthdays have been different. I think it is interesting how each birthday is different from the last. Our dear Lord made this day just for me by letting me be born. Over my 63 years I have been blessed to be remembered. This is why I try to remember all of theirs. Birthdays have always been special to me but I also remember the years when it seemed that everyone forgot. I was so depressed that I said I would not let this happen again. I even baked my own cake one year! Now I let them know by saying "Big day coming up" Then they remember fast. This is my gentle way to remind them that this is so important to me. I am still here because the Lord wants me here. He still has work for me to do on this earth.

OUR BIG TEST OF FAITH

Our big test of faith happened in the year 2002. It all started in the month of July. That is when Bob's heart trouble took a turn for the worse. One sign of this change was when he finished his exercise at the gym, he was very tired. He was also having difficulty breathing. I called the heart doctor and he wanted him in the hospital right away. On July ninth he was admitted to the heart unit. His doctor ordered a heart catheterization to be done right away. Our doctor did not like what he found. He had two blockages of 95%. This was not good news. He could have a heart attack at any time. Meanwhile; I called my prayer group so our prayer chain could be started; as we know the power of prayer. We had to make the right decision on what to do next. He was going through a lot. The heart team was very good to us. I knew that in the morning, the nurses are busy doing many things to him, so I did not go early to see him. I didn't know that the doctor would be in early to see him and to talk with him so I went to mass first. Bob's doctor called me and told me that he had to have open-heart surgery, Bob said he wanted to talk to me first. Dr Snyder told me that he had to have this operation or he would have more trouble, possibly heart damage if we wait. He told us that one of the best surgeons had an opening on Friday. This meant major surgery before Bob could go home. Bob had made up his mind even before I arrived. He knew it had to be done. When I got to the hospital things were in motion for a Friday surgery. Everything was happening so fast. I felt that this had to be. I was thanking the Lord that Bob had a good doctor taking care of him. It was also a blessing that this spot was open for him.

I had to get a hold of the family so they could see him before the surgery. So much was happening, so fast. We needed prayers. On Thursday the family came to see him. Everyone made the effort to come to see him. There were many things to be done to prepare for his surgery. The nurses explained just what would happen. This was all new to us. I was at the hospital by 6 am so I could be with him before he went for surgery. Each step was discussed before it happened. It was hard to say goodbye this time. It would be a long surgery and very risky. Many things could happen. While I was waiting I decided to call the kids and let them know what was happening. I had to go outside to use my cell phone. I stayed at the hospital waiting for the doctor to tell me that it was all over. I had time to pray and hope for the best. The nurse came and told me it would be at least four more hours so I could go out for a walk. I did talk to my friend, Rose, who is always home. She offered to come up but I told her it was going to be a long one. The waiting room was filled with other families waiting to hear about their loved ones. Everyone was working, so I was waiting alone but knowing that Jesus was at my side, helped me get through it. Bob Jr. had his big tennis tournament at Lehigh College but he came when he could. Time passed slowly. The nurse came out and told me to go for lunch that it would be awhile yet. I also needed to walk. It was hard just sitting there. Finally Dr Wu came out and told me that Bob was in recovery. He told me that he had repaired his blockage but his heart was enlarged from hypertension for many years. He would then be moved to the heart unit but visiting is only fifteen minutes per hour. He said that the nurse would come and get me when I could see him.

The surgery went well but it was still a long road ahead. The nurses were with him all the time. When I went in, I saw all kinds of tubes hanging everywhere, connected to all kinds of machines. He was in a lot of pain and very tired. I could see that I had a big cross to carry. I prayed "Dear Jesus you have taken my Bob into the darkness and the unknown with this surgery. I know that you will bring him back into the light and show him what path to take this time. Lord this is for your honor and glory. Please send your healing power on him. I know that I am being tested too, by what I have to do to help him get well. He is in your hands, Oh Lord I pray. I'm sure that you are using him to reach others. I know that he is suffering now and he has a long journey to go. Help us all to come closer through this trial. Amen"

Here it is July 14th 2002. Bob is into his second day after surgery. It was very hard to see Bob looking so gray. He had his eyes closed but I could see that he was in pain. He could not talk but he could move his head. By the next visit he was given three pints of blood because he had lost so much. He was on morphine for pain. It changed his personality.

I visited with him on Saturday with James and then we went to his house for lunch. I returned at 1 pm. We had a good visit this time for twenty minutes. Then I went for tea and a muffin and returned at three pm. Bob still could not talk. His throat was so dry. He was very tired so I said I would be back in a little while that I had a few things to do. I did not say when I would be back. I missed the five pm visit and Bob was upset with me. He said I was not there all day. He had the nurses calling all over trying to find me. All I did was go home to pick up my meds. In his mind, he thought I was gone a long time. He was so mixed up. I believe the drugs had something to do with it. Then when I did come he had one order after another for me.

As I reached for his water cup, I hit his chest collector box, which was on the floor, and I went flying onto the floor. I tried to get my balance and my finger went right through his water cup. It seems funny now, but it didn't at the time. I had pain in my leg. The nurse got me some ice. This was one of many battles we would have. He was very upset with everything. I did not feel like I wanted to be there. I could just walk away. He had to stay in the heart unit for a little longer. There was no room for him in the other unit yet. This just made things harder. I prayed "Oh Lord give me the strength that I need to get through this."

All the children came to visit him. That helped me get over some of the stress. Aunt Rose took me to lunch and Terri came along too. Bob is now in the Transitional Heart Unit. He looks much better. His blood is low so he may have to get more blood. All his tubes are out now except the heart monitor so he can now walk around. He has no appetite. But this too shall pass.

"Thank You Jesus" for all that you are doing with us right now. All of our friends are praying to you to make Bob well again. It is good to have this support. Bob took two walks yesterday and one today, to get to his room. He is trying real hard to get well. He did not sleep well. Somehow, we will get past this trial, like all our others; through the power of prayer.

It is now July 16th, 2002. Dan Thompson stopped by to give Bob communion but he could not receive it yet so he just prayed with him. It was so thoughtful of him to come. We are so blessed to have good friends. Thinking back, I remember the second day I was sitting in the waiting room, I got a call from our friends, the Caulfield's, who were on vacation in Hawaii. They said that they had got a voice message saying something was wrong with us. It is so good to have people who care about us like that. I was not supposed to use the cell in the hospital but I did not know it at that time. It interferes with the machinery. Sometimes it is good to have quiet but not in the hospital. We will make it through this rough time. This I know for Jesus told me so.

After we got home I did not have time to spare for I had to put on my nurse's hat to help Bob for there was a lot to do. It was two weeks today that Bob had his surgery". Thank you Lord for sending good people to take care of us. Thank you for guiding the surgeon's hands". This is a hard time for Bob who did not want to carry this cross. But he is doing better every day. I know he is in Jesus' hands.

"Dear Jesus we are waiting for Fr. Dadoni to bring us the Eucharist so we can get stronger in you; so that we can do your work whatever it may be". I hope to get back to daily mass next week. Bob was waiting anxiously for Fr. Dadoni to come. He didn't come until 11:30. By then Bob had given up on him. Bob made the statement" that it must not be important to receive". So I know he was feeling blue. So I began to pray that he would come soon. Almost as soon as the angry words came out there was a knock on the door. It was Fr. Dadoni. Fr. asked me to leave them alone so Bob could go to confession. Bob was happy after he left.

Right now he has congestion in his chest, he is uncomfortable with that. I called the doctor but they were all away. It was Friday and I got the answering service. Finally I got a doctor who was on call. He told me to give him Robitussin for his cough. The end of another busy day!

Saturday, July 27th, 2002. Today he seems to be better. The doctor has him on some new medications. We are doing our walks together but he wants to go too far. But that is the way Bob always is. Thank you Jesus for another day. It was a hot day and we wanted to get our walk in early. We are doing well with that. Praise the Lord.

I went shopping today to get a few things that we needed, plus I returned a scale that I bought while Bob was in the hospital. He didn't like it. Bob wants to get back to making the baskets as he is bored, but I hope he is not getting into it too quick. "Thank you Jesus for your help."

It is now July 30th. This past weekend was tough for Bob, due to the congestion in his lungs. He went to the doctor yesterday. Today he is having his lungs x-rayed. Some fluid is showing up. He may have to have his lungs tapped. He goes to Rehab for his heart today to see what program he will be on. He is doing better today. This is the first day he has had a "sense of humor". His appetite is coming back too. It is very hot out today so we walked inside the hospital to stay cool.

Annette and Kirk came to visit us today for they were away on vacation when this happened. Diane had her in and out visit. She has lots of work to do with her home business and her day job. Cory came over for the weekend and James and Liz came by. My friend, Jan, came to see him too. So now we wait until the doctor calls to see where we are going from here. Bob's sisters have been calling to see how he is doing. They came last week for a visit and brought him a fruit basket, which was really nice. Bob loves fruit. I got the nurses some candy for all the care they gave him while he was in the hospital. We dropped it off on one of our trips to Allentown.

Well, here it is August 2, 2002. Three weeks since Bob's surgery but he is looking a lot better. The cough that he has is hard on him. The weather doesn't help either. We walked in the mall yesterday and it went really well. Bob is working with the baskets again. This helps to keep his mind occupied. He's sleeping now, so this helps him get the rest he needs.

We like the South Mall for it has a walking path. This is part of his physical therapy. Thank you dear Jesus for being with us on this journey. I am going to daily mass again for Bob is good enough to leave alone for a little while.

August 3rd, Saturday. Where did this week go? Bob is pushing too much with the exercise already. I can hardly wait for the time when Bob can drive the car himself. He wants me to go his way and to drive that way too. It is very stressful for me. Everything I do is wrong. But he did like the soup that I made. He is going to have a hard time following a "healthy heart program". He is so fussy about how stuff is cooked.

He will be going for rehab now. This means more driving in the car. He still has that awful cough and now he is having some trouble sleeping.

August 9th we went for our walk this morning. It was so hot out. It is not good to walk in this heat. Bob had no hat on his head. I was very angry because he would not listen about the hot sun. So I walked home by myself. I hope he realizes what he is doing to both of us.

"Dear Jesus please help him forgive me for my anger". He thinks I am stubborn now. He is taking the car to go get a haircut and he is not supposed to even be driving yet. Bob still has the dry cough, it hurts when he coughs. He tries to hide it, but I know he should go to see the doctor, but he says "No, I'll see him next week". I watch in silence. He still does not sleep well. Maybe when he gets to Rehab things will be better. Except that I will have to drive him. That always means a fight, as he tells me how to drive and where. This is a hard cross to bear. Fortunately, we don't have to travel far in the car. If this is what we need to do to get him well, then let it be. "Thank you Jesus for sending your healing power on us.

It is four weeks since Bob's surgery. I just returned from church and the drug store. Bob went for his walk while I was gone. He is having a lot of trouble with this dry cough, which the doctor told him is coming from a nerve that was cut during surgery. This is just a side effect of the open-heart surgery. He still has some fluid on his lung, which is supposed to go away slowly.

August 12th, one month since his surgery and Bob is almost back to his old self. God has been so good to us. Bob started Rehab today so now we'll see what gets healed now. Our friends have been very kind in bringing us food so I don't have to cook every night. He is slowly getting his appetite back. It was good to get to mass in the morning again. It is going to be a hot week. We'll go back to the mall for our walks. I hope to get back to the club for my exercise soon. Diane is going away for a few days with Cory and her brother Dave. They are going to the Maryland shore. We have not seen Jim in a couple of weeks. He has a busy life style. Everything is moving along. "Thank you Lord Jesus for working in our life".

Here it is August 19th and Bob went to Rehab by himself. It has been a better week since Bob is driving himself. I had a bad weekend of headaches and dizziness. I guess my allergies are acting up.

"Thank you Jesus, it is August 21st and your healing power is working. Help Bob to listen to the warning of what is good for his heart".

August 22nd. It is our 43rd Anniversary and we are still together! We had a quiet dinner at a local restaurant. For what God has joined together, let no man part. Our promises that we made to each other were true and forever until death due us part. Over the years we have had some rough waters but like most storms they pass by. We can make it easier if you try again to be good to each other. It was a nice day. Our wedding day of so many years ago was filled with joy and happiness. May we have many more. With God on our side, we will make it. "Thank you Jesus for this day and your many blessings. Amen".

August 30th-Well Lord it has been a busy week, as you know. We had some ups and downs. I have been sick myself. Please help me figure out what to do about my reflux illness. I stopped taking my meds because of the cost. But what I am taking is not working. I will have to go back on the good stuff.

Bob had a bad day this week and I thought to myself "Here we go again". But it worked out. "Dear God help me with my thinking for I am having a rough time remembering. Thank you for Cory showing his love. Please work in his life for he is trying hard. Watch over his Mom and Dad in their relationship with each other. Help them in their healing of dealing with each other and Cory. Thank you for being with us all. Thank you for being with me and Dave while driving to Philly when he had to get his eyes checked. Praise the Lord for the rain this week. It was a dry summer and we needed the rain. Praise the Lord. Thank you for answering our prayers. Thank you for working with us at this time and always."

September 1, 2002

Yesterday was a very interesting day. Bob was his old self again. Praise the Lord! He wanted to take a long ride to the flea market. He also needed to get more work from Diane. I was dragging behind but I made it. He is back to his teasing and joking around. He played his card games on the computer. He was also watching football again; all the old stuff that he enjoyed doing. I know that he is healing. It's the first of the month; a time of new beginnings. "Thank you Jesus for your healing power."

"Now I need you to heal my reflux disease. Thank you for finding information on the computer on how to write my book. I know I am on my way now. Thank you for my friend Bernice. She helped me to get started with my stories on paper. This is what the article said to do. I am taking that as a confirmation that you want me to do this. I needed this to get going. This book will be in your honor and glory. For you alone know where I am going with this. Amen"

Now it is Labor Day. It's a holiday that has changed a lot over the years. We went for a walk this morning. It is cool outside after two days of rain. The grass is green instead of brown. It really needed a drink of water. Father Paul talked long at Mass today. He talked about the real meaning of Labor Day and why we celebrate it. The fruits of your labor are what counts, not just your money. Many good things can come from whatever your job brings to you. Years ago we always had cookouts and family gatherings. Now it is just Bob and I. When you have your health you have a lot to be thankful for. Today is a beautiful day. It was good to be at Mass. Bob went for his walk while I was at Mass. He was busy making baskets for Diane when I came home. He seems to be happy doing this. He likes to keep busy. I work in a different way. Bob is doing well with his health right now. "Thank you Jesus for answering our prayers. Watch over us as we travel today."

September 7, 2002

Where did the weeks go? I did not log anything since Sept. 2 and here it is Sept. 7th. "Oh Lord, you have outdone yourself today". It is such a beautiful day, filled with sunshine. It was cool this morning when I went for my walk. It was so good to breathe the fresh air. I went to Mass and then stopped at my sister-in-law's house for tea and bagels. It was good to stop and share my happenings with her. Bob has been doing well with his exercises and basket making for Diane.

"Thank you Jesus for helping us to find our new home here. We are happy here and Bob says he will not move again. This part of our journey is still uncertain but you will let us know what we are to do. We thank you for our health. Please bless the Caulfields with a good trip to South Carolina. We will miss being with them this year. Today is Sunday, another sunny day but a little on the hot side. We went to Mass at 9 o'clock, then headed for Diane's. She wanted us to go out for lunch with her. John's parents came also. It was good to see them. The Eagles lost their game today. Bob was not happy about that. I have been working on the lesson for our prep program at church. Thank you Jesus for today.

Another beautiful day! Bob went to breakfast with his friends and I went to breakfast with my sister-in-law, Elva. She seemed to be so restless. The Lord needs to settle her down. Bob seems to be doing well so far. He is still doing the baskets for Diane. We went to her house again and then went to visit our friends, Sue and Joe Yost. They wanted us to see their new house. It was really nice to see them. Sue is going to have surgery tomorrow. She has a blockage from an old surgery. "Please dear Lord send your healing power down upon her. Let her know that you are with her always. Be with Joe for he is lost when she is not there. Keep him strong in his faith. Thank you Lord for reaching out to others".

September 16, 2002

Today is the first day that Bob is going to Rehab by himself. He is doing quite well". Thank you Lord that we have Christopher for the weekend". It was good to share with him. He loves to be with Bob. Bob misses him when he is not around. "Please help my sister to heal from her breast cancer. She sounds very lonely. Help her find a new hobby that she can handle with all the time on her hands. Please open the doors allowing us to go to see her soon. It is a hot day today but thank you for the rain last night. It has been a very dry summer. Thank you for letting me get back on my meds. Diane loaned me some until I get my order. I know that I need them everyday. Thank you Lord for helping to heal me".

September 26, 2002

Here it is almost the end of September and we are being blessed with some gentle rain. We really need it". Thank you Jesus for blessing us with good friends". We visited with Sue and Joe yesterday. They have a lovely home. Sue is feeling much better now since her surgery; especially since no cancer has shown up.

Bob is doing well with his walks, plus he's watching what he eats and drinks. "Dear Jesus please send your healing power to my legs. I have had pain in them for a couple of weeks now. Also, please help Diane to make the right decisions in her life. Thank you for my new friend, Maria, who helps with the prep program in our church. Everything I do is in your name, Jesus."

October 5, 2002

It is the day after my birthday and all is quiet today. Bob is at work and I am all alone. It's good to be alone sometimes. "Thank You for letting us have time together on vacation this week. It was three days of doing just what we felt like doing; taking walks, watching ball games, taking a car ride to see the wild ponies by the Maryland shore, and going to our favorite Italian restaurant. We have been there many times so we know where to go. We saw a kite contest while walking on the beach. We enjoyed the beautiful shore. Thank You Lord."

October 6, 2002

Back to routine and going to heart therapy for Bob. "Thank you for having family with me on my birthday". For my birthday, we went out for dinner with my two sisters-in-law and then came back to play cards at Rory's house. We had a fun time. When we got back from our trip, there was a box on the doorstep from our sister-in-law in Florida. It was nice to get a present from someone so far away. She had made some pillows and a pillow for our sofa. It was nice of her to give a gift of her talents. Her note inside said "Thank you for all the work that we did for her last year when she moved from one house to another". She was thankful for us being with her at this hard time in her life. So much has happened since that time that I can hardly believe it. Time flies by so fast. It is good to enjoy each day at a time.

We now have a new car. This is Bob's pride and joy. It is a three year old Caddy but Bob likes it a lot. All of our children were out of town for my birthday except James so he is having us over for steak dinner tonight. Diane is in New York and I did not hear from Dave so I guess he forgot too. Bob Jr. is in Maryland with his family this weekend so I didn't see them either. Birthdays do change one year to the next. This was just a "Senior Moment", feeling sorry for myself. I know that it is the day the Lord has made us so we should be glad with him. He has called us to be part of His family. At 66 I am glad to have people that love me. My prayer group sent cards and the family did too. So—it was all good.

October 14, 2002

Christopher was here. It's always a good weekend when Christopher comes to see us. He told Pop Pop how much he loves him and me too. He kept saying how we spoil him because we do things he likes to do when he comes. We let him have his friend, Ian, come for a sleep over. They are so well behaved when they are together. "Thank You Jesus for the love. Amen"

October 15, 2002

It is a fresh fall morning. We had a slight frost last night. The house has a chill to it. It is soon time to put the heat on. "Thank You Lord for another day to serve you. Be with my Cory as he wants to receive you in his heart. Please open the doors to him that he can receive you soon. Please help my grandson get to know what he needs to know in order to receive you. You set me on fire the day I received you. Please let him have this joy soon. This I pray. Ashley has been waiting a long time too. Please open the doors for these children so they will be able to serve you. Their souls are hungry for you. Please let their souls be filled with Your holy bread."

Bob went to our family doctor today. Everything is good with him. He and I both got a flu shot. I hope we have a good winter. Bob made chicken soup. He likes to share with his sisters. He loves to cook. We had Elva over for supper. We are taking care of the "widows."

At our prep program we had a video on the Rosary. We played the bells and sang while praising God. "Thank You Jesus for the joys. We gave each child a rosary. They were thrilled to get them. Thank you for your spirit working in them all.

October 19, 2002. Today I will be going on a three-mile walk for the cancer fund. I've been awake since 3 am. I guess I am just excited. This is the third year that I did this. I really didn't think that I could do it again this year due to my knee problems. But I didn't want to miss this important walk. A lot of my friends will be there. "Thank You Jesus" for putting these good friends into my life. This year we are expecting 3,000 women to do this fundraiser for cancer. I have been training all summer for the walk. "Lord, I will put it in your hands. Praise Jesus, my friend". It was a cool, gray, rainy day. It was neat to be a part of so many women. Some ran, some were fast walkers, others walked slowly. That's where I fit in.

I was at the end of the line when I saw someone else struggling even harder than me. She needed my help. She said her name was Wendy and that her doctor had ordered her to do the walk. I gave her my hand and helped her up the hill. She was now my buddy for the walk. This was her first time on a walk of this kind. She had so much pain that she was crying. So we got talking about stuff and she told me that she is a professor from Penn State and that she teaches French. So I told her about my trip to France. We began to sing songs to pass the time away while walking. She started to sing Christian songs, then French, and then Jewish songs. She confided in me that she was Jewish. She acted like she knew me a long time. We talked and sang so much that we both forgot about our pain. We both walked over the finish line at the same time. It was an interesting walk and I will probably never see her again. But it was good that you used me Lord. She never would have finished without my help.

On the last lap, another lady came up to me, when she saw me walking with Wendy, she asked me if I remembered her. She helped me with the first graders at St Joseph church where I taught the children how to play the bells and to sing praise to the Lord. For this woman to remember me teaching the bells; confirms that I should continue teaching the children how to use the bells and praise the Lord during prayer time.

We always celebrate after the walk. All my prayer group friends were waiting for me at the end of the line to cheer me along. It is a great feeling to finish even if I am the last one.

Love of human beings, to give of themselves, was the instigating factor of this walk. This love was instilled in them by God to help raise funds to find a cure. Little did I know that this would be my last walk for cancer due to problems with my knees.

October 27, 2002

Christopher came for the weekend again. It was Halloween. We have Trick or Treat on Sunday in our area. Rachel came with Bob so she went along too. I decided to get into my clown outfit and go with them. A lot of people sit on their porch to give out candy and greet the children. Some children were even giving out the candy. After we made our rounds we came back and gave our candy out. The kids had fun doing that.

Bob was at a work meeting all day so he wanted to watch football. So I took Christopher home and Pam picked up Rachel. She had a Girl Scout meeting. My friend, Jan, came to visit us so I made a meal for everyone. Bob took Katie to work at Dorney Park. She was in a rush to get going. I was happy to have everyone here.

October 28, 2002

Today was cold, but I still managed to get some walking in while Bob was at Rehab. This is Bob's last week with this program. He will be back at his club for a new program. We stopped to get some apples on the way home. We also had to drop off some things that Christopher left at my house. He does his work from his house now so he was too busy to talk to us. We took that with a grain of salt.

November 1, 2002

It is Bob's last day at Rehab. He will still exercise at his club. I had x-rays taken of my back, hips, and knees because of all the pain I have been having. It's all arthritis. I will have to learn to live with it and learn to manage my pain.

While I was at Mass, I was sitting in back of one of my students. He gave me a big hug before he left Mass. This was like a "Thank You" for teaching him. This is a bonus from the Lord. "Thank You Lord for your love coming from others. You are so good."

NEW SPECIAL MONTH

Let us slow down LORD for your special day will soon be here. Christmas is one of my favorite times of the year. We do have to take the time to enjoy each and every moment that we are with other people sharing all the joys that the holidays can bring. We try to remember JESUS that you are the reason for the season. Each card we send out goes with a note of love to that person. Jesus has shown us over the years that some things can wait during this time for another day to be done. For what is really important that we spend time with our loved ones. This year's celebration with my prayer group was really neat. We started with by going to Mass and a prayer time together and then we had our party. It is so different than any other Parties we go to. Jesus has top billing with us. Thank you for the gift of the snow for it just made it more fun. We wished each other joy for all our families too. For the next time we would be together would be a New Year. It was snowing on Christmas day. This meant that not everyone would be coming to our house. Some made it early and we shared with them. We did have dinner with those who could be with us. The snow was piling up, so some of the family called to say that they could not make it. This was better to do than for them to get stuck somewhere on the highway. We did get the news that there would be two new babies born next year. One would be our first great grand child and one would be my son David's first child, so now it would be seven grandchildren and one great grandchild. Our family tree is growing again which brings us joy. The year of 2002 had many ups and downs but we made it again. It is all in GOD'S hands. Bob's birthday is the last day of the year but we celebrated on the 30th so we could be all together for him. We welcomed in the New Year with going to mass for it is a HOLY day for us. Thanks for all the blessing of this year and our new health. We do all these things in your name dear JESUS as you walk each day with us all. Amen.

NEW ENGLAND 2002, OUR DAYS OF THANKS

On November 27, 2002 we were headed for New England to spend the Thanksgiving Holiday with my sister, Doris, and her family. This is the first time that I've been back for a holiday in 35 years. We had good weather for our trip but the morning after we arrived, it started snowing. Cousin George was making a skating rink for his children in his back yard. It was neat to watch them. It was so good to see all the family again. We are always greeted with love and respect. Bob and Doris couldn't wait to get started on their card games.

My other sister's son lives next door to Doris. We see them a lot when we are here. Even though the snow was on the ground it was cold outside but it was nice and cozy in the house. "Thank You Lord for the safe trip in our new car". Diane called to make sure that we got there safe and sound. It was good to hear her voice. "God, please bless them at home and bring them closer together on this holiday. Also, thank you for healing my sister, Doris, of cancer. She still gets very tired during the day but this is normal after surgery.

Our Thanksgiving Day started with the smell of two turkeys roasting in the oven. We needed two turkeys to feed 36 people coming for dinner. We all helped to put up tables and decorate them with red tablecloths and a centerpiece. Doris had the baking done by the time we arrived. Between the smells from the kitchen and the snow on the ground it was just like an old fashioned Thanksgiving. It reminded me of the song" Over the River and Through the Woods to Grandmother's House We Go" Everyone brought something to contribute to the feast. We had a wonderful meal.

Everyone wants to know how everyone else is. We have a lot of catching up to do. My sister is a wonderful hostess. She makes everyone feel at home. It was so nice to see everyone. Our cousins didn't want us to go home because we always find time to do fun things with them. Sunday night my nephew treated us to a Pizza Party. That was neat! Everyone was glad to know that Doris was healing from her surgery in August.

Bob went for a walk in the cold, which is not good for him to do. But, he won't listen to me. He never does anything in a small way. It is now November 30th. It is a gray day and the snow is melting. We will be going home in a couple of days. I have been practicing on the computer. I get better everyday. Bob plays cards with Doris so she is enjoying his visit too. It will be hard to say "goodbye" especially since we are getting older. We are blessed to have such happy times together. We never know when we will see each other again.

On December 5th we headed home. The weather was good. There was a lot of work waiting for us when we got home. While we were gone we had a painter paint our house. Surprise, surprise! He thought we were coming home the following day. What a mess we walked into. He was not finished, so we couldn't sleep in the house due to the smell of the paint. I called my sister-in-law and she said we could sleep at her house for the night.

The walls looked so nice and clean when he was finished. Bob could hardly wait to get started on the gift baskets that he does for Diane. He really enjoys doing it. God has been so good to us to let us be helpful at this time in our lives. I am glad to be back to working on my own computer, which is one of my hobbies. Before you know, we will be getting ready for Christmas, which is my favorite holiday.

THE WITNESSING

Time: this is a word that everyone uses at one time or another. Webster's Dictionary says a lot about this word. Time is: an interval, a period of time, often a span of time, an opportune or designated moment, the rate of speed of a measured activity, the beat of musical rhythms; installment buying; to set time for a schedule; to regulate for orderly; sequence to record the speed of duration.

Time—what is time? It is how we pass by on earth. I feel time is a very special gift from God. Everyone has to deal with it. However; we can do what we want with this gift. There is only 24 hours in a day. Our time to be born and our time to die are chosen by our good Lord. But we get to choose what we do with the time between being born and dieing. There are many things to enjoy. Some people waste energy. Others plan days that slip by quickly, others who have to spend eight hours working. Some time is spent eating and sleeping, exercising, and praying each day.

Did you ever think about what you should be doing with your time? Twenty four hours sounds like a long time but it isn't when you think of all you have to do in a day. To enjoy the beauty of life you must work real hard at it. Learning to manage our time is a good thing. If we spend time on anger, stress, and loneliness time can seem endless. I used to be crabby when I first woke up. It was a terrible way to start the day. I asked the Lord to heal me. I had to change the way I started my day. I started to pray first thing in the morning. This brought me joy. I wanted every moment filled with time well spent. I found that my days could be happy by making time to be with Jesus first. I had to make time to be happy. When I started to give myself to others each day I set myself free to enjoy the precious gift of time with joy.

There is also a thing called quality time. One example is when you make an extra effort to see the sun coming up in the morning to realize that I am alive for another day. It is like the caterpillar leaving the cocoon to become a butterfly; another beautiful creature that God has made for us to enjoy. How much time does it take for a caterpillar to become a butterfly? Books can tell you that. All good things take time.

I hope you start to enjoy your freedom, of time, by looking for the gifts that nature has made to us. God, in his master plan made it just for you and me. Take time to enjoy the star filled nights. Enjoy the dew on the grass in the early morning. Take time to smell the roses. Listen to the birds singing. It is a wonderful sound. Our world is filled with many beautiful things for us to enjoy but we have to take the time to enjoy them. Life is too short to waste this gift of time. There is a time to laugh, to cry, to play, to work, to travel, time to share with friends, time to have fun, time to talk and a quiet time for prayer. Did you ever think how important time really is? It becomes very important to a mature person who is retired. I know; for I have done it all and I am still going strong because God has planned this for me. I enjoy everyday one day at a time. There's that word again. Now we know what a gift time is. Time is the most important thing created by God outside of humans made in his image and likeness.

THE SPIRITUAL GIFT OF A RAINBOW—MANY I HAVE SEEN

I love rainbows; I know it is God's way of saying "here I am." A rainbow is a gift of nature bright and shining in the sky after a storm has gone by. Everyone gets excited when they see one. To me, each color tells me a story. Red is for the joys in my life. Yellow is for the laughter along our journey with friends and family. Blue is for the times of unknowing adventures. Orange is for the many maybes along the way. Purple is for the sadness which comes with the ups and downs along our paths of life. Green is marked for the growth in our spirituality. Last is the, gold which shows us the brightness of the treasures shared with our Christian friends; believing in God's promise that we will receive our reward of eternal life. We are all part of his great plan; for we are his chosen ones.

NEW ENGLAND, JULY 2003

We were going to New England to see my sister, Doris. We took Cory and Christopher. Diane was driving us in her van. I really didn't want to go on this trip without Bob but he didn't want to go. My sister had planned a Lobster party for the Fourth of July holiday. Diane said she wanted to leave by 7 am so I went to pick up Christopher at 6 am. I should have known better. She didn't come until 10 am. This was our first delay. More delays came from people coming from the mountains. Once we got through there it was ok. It was a very hot day and of course the boys were always hungry and thirsty. Diane was upset with this road; she has no patience. She did not want to stop at rest areas but I made her. I cannot keep going without stopping. We finally reached the New York part called Route 84. From then on, it was clear sailing. The boys kept asking, "Are we there yet, where are we, how long now?" I kept pointing out things but they were too busy playing games and they were not interested.

We finally pulled into my sister's yard at 4 pm. Everyone was eating lobster and clams for dinner, but they all took the time to come and greet us. They were so glad that we were there. My sister had a band playing in the yard. Her granddaughter was the lead singer in the band. She has a beautiful voice. She did a good job.

We just sat down and joined dinner. Everything was great. Doris worked so hard on this party. She had 80 people there. She shared with me that her husband, George once said, "You should have a good party before your wake as a party without you there would be no fun". She was even dancing at the end before everybody started to leave. It was a neat affair and one that we will not forget. Bob missed it all.

Doris was busy with her guests, which was alright with us. We found lots of people to talk to. Everyone was looking for Bob. He was really missed. The boys headed for the pool after the long, hot ride in the car. They were busy with their cousins. It was good to see the family again. Diane was enjoying herself too. She was relaxing in the pool and reading a book. I called Bob to let him know that we got here safely. He sounded like I was boring him. So I only called two more times and that was it.

Diane went to the beach one day but I stayed with Doris, as I came to be with her. We had a peaceful day until they all came back from the beach. My niece took the kids to the park one day; which they enjoyed. Before we knew it, it was time to head for home. Four days went by so fast! My sister is feeling much better now. I was so happy to be able to visit with her. I don't know when I will ever get back there again. I'm very tense traveling in a car. I wish I could get over this fear but it is something deep inside me. I forget who really is taking care of me. I'll remember this next time. Thank you Lord for letting us get together again. God was watching over us on our trip.

THE DOMINICAN RETREAT 2003—MY LAST TIME THERE

We were only home for three days when I left again for my annual retreat to the Dominican Retreat House in Elkins Park in May of 2003. This is where I go every year to be alone with Our Lord Jesus.

My dear friend, Annamae, picked me up as we only have one car now. We also had to pick up another woman on the way. We all had lots to share on the way down. We talked about how all our families were doing and how the Lord has been working in our lives since we last saw each other. The messages were "loud and clear" as to the road I am to take. I came with a heavy heart but I knew it would be lighter going home. It was so good to be with my friends from St Paul's and all the friends that I have made through the years at the Retreat House.

Upon arriving at the Retreat House, I realized that I had a room to myself. This made me very relaxed knowing that I didn't have the responsibilities that I had in the past. For this year was different. I am no longer a "promoter", inviting other people to come. I was a retreat person just like everyone else. It was a different feeling, a good feeling. I was free to be myself. Also, I had no meetings to attend. This left me more time to pray and listen to God with my whole mind and heart. I felt free to be with Jesus at my own pace. Our prayer group met at Our Lady of Lordes Shrine to pray like we do every year. We pray and thank Our Lady for all She has done to help us over this past year. Many changes have taken place at the Retreat House, all for the good of the house.

Many sisters are older now and have left to do other things. It was good to share with all our prayer friends from my past life. The program has been shortened and also changed for the better. New people are doing the work that the sisters did in the past. Our cups runneth over with joy to be sharing our faith with so many others.

The" sharing" on Saturday night was very different too. There were three new people who were willing to share how they came here for the first time. Dotty and Judy have been working as a team doing a good job of "promoting" people to answer their call to meet JESUS.

Everybody goes on vacation to rest, but resting in the arms of JESUS is the best one. His love is flowing from each person here in all kinds of ways. All the time spent with God's people while in his kingdom is so important. We are on Holy ground and we walk with wings on our feet. Many have come to open their hearts to God and receive so many blessings. We feel the Holy Spirit doing His good works in each and every person.

Our retreat priest was a very interesting person, with a great sense of humor. He's a "down to earth" kind of person. We learned a lot from him. He made us laugh a lot but when he was teaching he had a serious side to him. We were there to learn and we did receive a great lesson in our faith. Our last Mass ended our two and a half days of time well spent with the Lord. I was again ready to face the world. I know Jesus is always with me so I have no fears of where I am going or what I am going to do. Praise the Lord! Amen

SANTA CAME TO OUR CHRISTMAS PARTY

It was Christmas time 2005. My prayer group has been getting together to pray for 35 years. At Christmas time we plan a special time together. We start by attending Mass and then praying together. We have shared many things with each other over these many years. We have always been there for each other. When a need for prayer comes along everyone is called to share that need for God's help. This has kept us strong together.

Other years in the past we would all prepare food for breakfast and have it at someone's home but now we are all getting older and it became harder to do this. We also exchanged gifts and cards at this time. This tradition was always a joyful time like all good things, but we wanted to change it to make it easier for all of us. We felt that the money spent on our gifts could be given to a needy family in our church so this is what we all wanted to do. We figured being with each other was gift enough. Then we talked about what family we could help.

We ended up going out for breakfast. We were all sitting there trying to pick out what we wanted; looking for the Senior Specials. All 12 of us were sitting there having a good time, trying to think about what would be good to eat. Two men were sitting near by and heard us talking. One came over and said "you look like you are having a good time". We explained that this was our Christmas party and that we just came from church. He said "maybe you would like to come and play cards with us this afternoon", kidding around. That was where they were going. They told us to enjoy our breakfast and Merry Christmas and then walked away. The waitress came to take our orders and said that we shouldn't worry about specials because one of the men was paying all your bills. "Well, I said how much is champagne"? We thought she was joking but she said that it was true. After placing our orders we called out to the man "thank you, Santa. He just smiled and waved to us. When he was done eating he came back over and told us that he could tell that we must all be mothers. Since he did not have a mom anymore to give a Christmas present to he decided to treat us. We said we would pray for him and his friend. We knew he had some health problems.

It just goes to show that it is better to give than it is to receive. We gave our gifts up for the poor and we received the free food. Then we did not have to pay so we all left the waitress a big tip so she was given a gift too. What a neat way to share the joys of giving just like Jesus wants us to. Our Lord sent us his love and we shared it and so did Santa. Jesus said "what ever you do in my name you will be blessed".

A SPIRITUAL DREAM 2004

One night I had a spiritual dream. It was two days before we were to leave for our trip to Florida. In my dream, I had seen Pope John at a meeting. I was sitting there with two other priests. They were talking about closing our school! Then I was at Mass and the Pope was blessing us. I received a gift from his Holiness. I knelt down to kiss his ring and he gave me a cross.

That same day we had visited with our brother-in-law, Andy, who was on his deathbed. He had been very sick for the past eight weeks. We have been praying for him everyday. He had lost a lot of weight and looked very thin in his bed. I had a feeling that the dream meant that we should be with him for he was carrying the cross. Maybe this meant that he had more to bear yet. My sister-in-law told me that she was praying the prayer card that I had sent to her since Andy was so sick. It was a prayer to St. Theresa. This has made her stronger. Our Lord does use our sleeping time to reach us. Now our dear Pope John has gone to his reward with Jesus. He is no longer suffering. He truly was a good shepherd to us all. God is so good. He shows us the way even in our dreams.

POPE JOHN PAUL II AND THEN LITTLE ME 2005

Jesus said "come follow me, I will make you fisher of men". Jesus was talking to all of us. This is how I know that I gave my book the right title, MY PRECIOUS CHILD, COME FOLLOW ME. This book was written to show how powerful prayer has been in my life. Pope John Paul, II loved being with children and so did I. My vocation was marriage and raising a family. But church and His people were always very important to me also.

On my last vacation I read a book about Pope John Paul called Rise Let Us Be On Our Way, which I enjoyed very much. First of all Pope John Paul, II has been a great person, who I have loved all these years; knowing how he loved people. He had lots of trials in his young life and so did I. He lost his mother at an early age and so did I. We both went on retreats. I found them to be so fulfilling. It was my home away from home. My retreat house was walking on holy ground. My cup was overflowing with the love I wanted to share with others since the Holy Spirit came to me.

My time spent in Lourdes, France with our Blessed Mother was so special to me. Pope John felt the same way about Mary. He was devoted to her and to the Rosary, just as I am. Pope John had his Bishops to share with and I had my prayer group. We all shared the Holy Spirit who has enlightened us over these many years in our everyday life as Jesus' followers. We have learned a lot from each other and from our church teaching as well. I have had a lot of trust in the Guardian Angels and the Saints. My marriage took place on August 22, 1959, which is Mary's feast day when she went to heaven. We shared the blessings of the church on our wedding day, with Mary smiling down on us.

For me, many changes in my faith have taken place but I am still hanging in there because God has led me to know good faithful people. Each year I am stronger. Just like Pope John, who went to Mexico to learn about Our Lady of Guadalupe and Juan Diego, I also went there to learn of the great faith that these people had. As a mother, grandmother, and wife I have many duties to perform in the name of Christ.

Daily mass is how I like to start my day; placing in prayer what I carry in my heart for others. When my "nest became empty" I found myself wanting to be with children again. This is how Grandma's Play Room came about; after much praying that I would make the right decision. I was asked to teach first graders at church. This was very rewarding for me. I learned even more about what God wanted me to do. Teaching children how to sing God's praise with "ringing bells" was a joy to my heart. The fruit of the spirit is our mission to spread the faith in all the work that we do. As a child, Pope John had St. Nicholas' stories told to him at Christmas time. I learned a lot about him while teaching the children. He was a very Holy man. In faith we did many things alike. Mother Theresa helped the poor all her life. Pope John met her many times, knowing that she was special; doing God's work.

I served with St Vincent De Paul Society for many years while working at St. Paul's church. Working with the Women's Group gave me a chance to lead them to many spiritual activities. We shared the work in Jesus' name. Bringing other's on retreat weekend was a calling to God's work. Working with the Dominican sisters showed me a great path to follow. This was a place where we could center on God and listen to his word with our hearts and souls. It was a little bit of heaven on earth. Pope John shared how when he was a bishop he was being a father to his people like St Joseph was to Jesus. He also helped me with many everyday problems over the years by praying to him. Pope John thought that celibacy would provide an opportunity to live out a type of fatherhood with chaste and dedication to Christ and His Virgin Mary. A priest can dedicate himself wholeheartedly to his pastoral duties. Christ remained celibate so he could dedicate himself totally to the service of God and man. My prayer book on the Blessed Sacrament has helped me spiritually in the presence of the Blessed Sacrament. God does exist. I have met Him. God has allowed me to meet the Sisters of Mercy at St Theresa's. They in turn, have led me to this book and prayer time with the Lord. Pope John met with other Bishops and we met in prayer with each other in love for each other in Christ. We gather strength from each other.

Making a retreat is a great gift from God. It is a time when everything else is put aside to encounter God and listen to Him alone. This is the most valuable exercise for someone on retreat. No one should be pressured to make a retreat. It is only experienced by free will. We who go on retreat have done the same thing as our beloved Pope John. He led retreats in the Vatican when he was a Cardinal. He has written many important papers. He realized how important Bishop's needed to be ready to speak of His faith. We all need to be ready too. If we know the truth it will set us free. We all encounter trials as part of our life of faith. "By the grace of God" is what gets us through it all. Pope John Paul has lived his faith so well. May he now rest in the peace of the Lord in his crowning glory for his job was well done. Someday I will be called home to be in His loving arms. For now I do what I can on this earth for I know that the power of God is with me always.

A CHILD SMALL WAS I (THE BELLS IN MY LIFE)

This story took place when I was about eight years old. I attended a catholic school, which was taught by sisters from Canada. They had some serious ways about them. Rules were rules and weren't meant to be broken; as I found out.

My teacher at this time had a little bell on her desk, which she rang when class was starting. This was a big temptation for me. I wanted to ring that bell so badly. When she wasn't looking, I rang the bell—ding, ding. Well, she called me up front and said "you don't ever ring that bell!" Then she got her ruler out and hit my hand for ringing the bell. I thought about that, long and hard and I never did ring that bell again.

I have to chuckle when I think about that because now I have my own bells to ring, a whole collection of them. I use them to teach children to praise and sing to the Lord. Now I can ring these bells all I want. My bells give joy to the children who play them. I feel that this is somehow connected to my past. I know I learned a lesson in my childhood, not to ring the bells without a good purpose and I found a good one teaching the children to praise the Lord with the bells. Ringing the bells has brought me joy for many years.

978-0-595-42993-(
0-595-42993-9

Printed in the United States
74496LV00004B/245

9 780595 429936